Essential Tagalog Grammar

Second Edition

A Reference for Learners of Tagalog

Fiona De Vos

Second Edition

ISBN 978-90-815135-4-8 (small paperback)
ISBN 978-90-815135-8-6 (grammar + 3 course books)

Also available in other formats:
ISBN 978-90-815135-1-7 (large hardcover)
ISBN 978-90-815135-2-4 (large paperback)
ISBN 978-90-815135-3-1 (ebook)

D/2011/Fiona De Vos, uitgever
NUR 630

learningtagalog.com
team@learningtagalog.com

Cover painting by Sabrina dei Nobili.

To my husband, Fre

Contents

Introduction

Essential Tagalog Grammar offers:
- clear, simple and concise explanations
- lots of practical examples focusing on everyday, informal Tagalog
- accurate definitions and translations
- pronunciation marks, with all long vowels (stress) and glottal stops indicated
- audio recordings of Tagalog sounds (downloadable from learningtagalog.com)
- extensive cross-referencing and a comprehensive index
- a simple well-organized format

Essential Tagalog Grammar includes:
- extensive alphabetical lists of noun, verb and adjective affixes with plenty of examples, useful for building vocabulary
- meanings of enclitic particles in context
- tables of markers and pronouns, question words, rules for indicating aspect, irregular verbs, numbers, time expressions and more
- lists of opening and closing particles and interjections
- clear explanations of the Point of Departure (the Tagalog "subject," "topic" or "focus") and the News (the Tagalog "predicate" or "comment"), markers and pronouns (Ang, Ng and Sa phrases), enclitic words and more

Essential Tagalog Grammar is recommended for:

- learners of Tagalog who want to understand how the language works and have a quick reference handy
- native speakers who want to gain insights into their own language
- anyone who wants to gain a deeper understanding of Tagalog grammar

Essential Tagalog Grammar is the ideal companion to Learning Tagalog: A Complete Course with Audio. The course is available at: learningtagalog.com

How to use this book

You can use this book purely as a reference, reading only the topics that interest you. The cross-references and the comprehensive index will guide you to related topics.

You can also read it from cover to cover, for instance, by doing one small section a day. After reading the book, you will have covered all the essential grammar points you need to speak and understand everyday Tagalog.

For a summary of the pronunciation symbols used in the book, see p. 24.

Exercises

After reading a section with one or more tables containing Tagalog and English phrases, you can do the following exercises:

- Cover up the column containing the English phrases and say the meaning of the Tagalog phrases.
- Cover up the Tagalog column, read the English phrases and say the Tagalog phrases.

What's new in this edition?

- improved explanations, definitions, translations and examples
- new example sentences and verb forms (aspects) added to all verb affixes
- new verb affixes, enclitic particle combinations and describing words
- a new section on the Tagalog POD vs. the English subject
- new example sentences added to some noun affixes and adjective affixes, and other topics
- new translations added to the chapters on pronunciation, forming and connecting words, and other topics
- new cross-references and index entries
- reorganized sections
- and more

Navigation tips for the ebook version

- In the Contents, click on a page number to go directly to a specific section.
- In the main text, click on a link or a page number to jump to a specific section.
- Click Alt+Left Arrow (Windows/Unix) or Command+Left Arrow (Mac OS) to return to the page you previously viewed.
- Click Ctrl+F/Command+F to search the ebook for a word or a phrase.

Contact

If you have any questions, comments or suggestions, you can contact the author at:

team@learningtagalog.com

Maraming salamat po'!

Pronunciation

Note: Downloadable audio recordings of Tagalog sounds and the pronunciation of the Tagalog words included in this chapter are available at: learningtagalog.com

Vowels and consonants

Vowels

The following vowels are used in native Tagalog words. The underlined vowels are long vowels.

vowel	examples	corresponding sounds in English	IPA symbols
a	<u>a</u>ga	*palm, about*	[a], [ə]
e	<u>e</u>re	*whey, dress*	[e], [ɛ]
i	<u>i</u>gi	*happy, kit*	[i], [ɪ]
o	<u>o</u>so	*row, thought*	[o], [ɔ]
u	<u>u</u>so, usa	*goose, put*	[u], [ʊ]

Consonants

The following consonants are used in native Tagalog words.

consonant	corresponding sound in English
b	*but*
d	*do*
g	*go*
h	*ham*
k	*cat*
l	*left*
m	*man*
n	*no*
ng	*ringing* [IPA symbol: ŋ]
p	*tip*
r	*run*
s	*sea*
t	*store*
w	*we*
y	*yes*

Note:

1. /k/, /p/ and /t/ are not aspirated, that is, there is no puff of air after them.

To hear the difference between aspirated and unaspirated sounds, say *kill* and *skill* out loud. In most dialects of English, /k/ is aspirated in *kill* and unaspirated in *skill*. Similarly, /p/ and /t/ are aspirated in *pill* and *till* but not in *spill* and *still*.

2. /ng/ can also be found at the beginning of a word in Tagalog (e.g. **ngayon** – *today, now*). You can practise the initial /ng/ sound by saying *ringing, ri...nging*.

Extra consonants for loan words

Tagalog makes use of additional consonants for loan words and names, borrowed mainly from Spanish and English. These are **c, f, j, ñ, q, v, x** and **z**. Examples:

Quezon City, computer.

Together with these extra consonants, the Tagalog alphabet is made up of 28 letters, i.e. the same 26 letters of the English alphabet, plus two letters—**ng** and **ñ**.

Letter names

The two Tagalog letters that are not found in the English alphabet are called *en gee* **(ng)** and *en yeh* **(ñ)**.

All the other letters have the same names as in English. Note that **z** is called *zee*, as in American English.

Diphthongs

diphthong	corresponding sound in English
ay	*wise*
ey	*whey*
oy	*boy*
uy	*too young*
aw	*now*
ew	*yeah why*
iw	*kiwi*
ow	*row*

How to pronounce /ll/ and /ñ/

letter(s)	pronounced as	examples	pronounced as
ll	ly	**Calle**	*"Calye"*
		Villegas	*"Vilyegas"*
ñ	ny (*"gn"* in *lasagna*)	**El Niño**	*"El Ninyo"*
		Los Baños	*"Los Banyos"*

Long vowels (stress) and glottal stops

Native Tagalog words are generally pronounced as they are spelled. *
The only things that are not represented in spelling are: (1) long vowels,
and (2) glottal stops [IPA symbol: ʔ] at the end of words.

An example of a glottal stop found in English is the sound represented
by the hyphen in *uh-oh!*

* Commonly-used exceptions to this are **ng** and **mga**, which are
pronounced as *"nang"* and *"manga,"* respectively.

Long vowels (stress)

In Tagalog, stressed syllables have a long vowel, while unstressed
syllables have a short vowel.

In this book, all syllables with a long vowel are underlined. Examples:

tra<u>ba</u>ho	*work, job*
<u>a</u>so	*dog*
ma<u>ka</u>ka<u>sa</u>ma	*will be able to come along*

It is important to make a distinction between long vowels and short
vowels to be clearly understood. For one thing, many words change
meanings when their long vowels are not clearly audible. Examples:

<u>bu</u>hay	*life*
buhay	*alive*

| mag-**aa**ral | *will study* |
| mag-aaral | *student, pupil* |

Optional long vowels

Vowels in syllables right before a pause, such as at the end of a sentence, may be made longer. Examples:

| Kumus*ta*?
Kumusta *na*? | *How are you? / How's it going?* |

These optional long vowels are not indicated in this book.

Final glottal stops

Some final vowels end with a glottal stop when followed by a pause (e.g. comma, period). When not followed by a pause, these vowels are elongated instead. In this book, these final glottal stops or long vowels are marked with the symbol /'/. Examples:

t**a**ma'	*right, correct*
hindi'	*not*
na**li**go'	*took a shower or a bath, washed (one's body)*

Pronunciation when used in a sentence:

| T**a**ma', hin*di* siya na**li**go'. | *Right, he/she didn't wash.* |

Note: When /'/ is not followed by a space, it represents one or more omitted letters, instead of a glottal stop or a long vowel. Examples:

b̲awa't	*each, every*
siya'y	*he/she's*
'yan	*that (near you)**

* See also: Clarification: near me etc. (p. 56)

Optional glottal stops

Technically, the following vowels begin with a glottal stop.

vowels	example	pronun-ciation	meaning
vowels at the beginning of a word	**a̲so**	"'a̲so"	*dog*
vowels following a hyphen	**mag-a̲ral**	"mag'a̲ral"	*to study*
vowels following another vowel	**maa̲ga**	"ma'a̲ga"	*early*

However, these glottal stops usually disappear in rapid speech.

Optional final /h/ sound

Final vowels that do not end with a glottal stop may be followed by a slight /h/ sound before a pause. Example:

Maa̲ga pa(h).	*It's still early.*

Summary of pronunciation symbols used

symbol	pronunciation
<u>underline</u>	long vowel
/'/ not followed by a pause*	long vowel
/'/ followed by a pause*	glottal stop

* pause – e.g. comma, period

Spelling system using diacritical marks

An official spelling system that uses diacritical marks for indicating long vowels and final glottal stops was introduced in 1939. Although it is used in some dictionaries and Tagalog learning materials, it has not been generally adopted by native speakers. The system is explained in Appendix A (p. 441).

Replaceable sounds

Replaceable vowel sounds

Some vowel sounds in native words can be replaced under certain conditions.

change	example	alternative pronunciation	meaning
from /i/ to /e/	la**la**k**i**	"la**la**ke"	*man, male*
from /e/ to /i/	sig**e** na	"sig**i** na"	*come on, please...*
from /o/ to /u/	t**o**tal	"t**u**tal"	*after all, anyway*

When the changes usually occur:

1. From /i/ to /e/: when /i/ is in the final syllable of a native Tagalog word that is followed by a pause*

example	alternative pronunciation	meaning
Gab**i**.	"Gabe."	*Evening.*
Itlog.	—	*Egg.*
Abr**i**l.	—	*April.*
Gab**i** na.	—	*It's already dark.*

2. From /e/ to /i/: when /e/ is in the final syllable of a word that is not followed by a pause*

example	alternative pronunciation	meaning
Sige na.	*"Sigi na."*	*Come on, please.*
Sige.	—	*OK.*
Perlas.	—	*Pearl.*
Eleksyon.	—	*Election.*

3. From /o/ to /u/: when /o/ is short (unstressed) and not followed by a pause*

example	alternative pronunciation	meaning
Ano pa?	*"Anu pa?"*	*What else?*
Botika'.	*"Butika'."*	*Drugstore.*
Biyolin.	*"Biyulin."*	*Violin.*
Ano?	—	*What?*
Bola.	—	*Ball.*

* pause – e.g. comma, period

Other replaceable sounds

sounds	may be replaced by	example(s)	alternative pronunciation(s)	meaning
ai	*ay, ey, e*	ka**i**lan	"ka*y*lan, ke*y*lan, k**e**lan"	*when*
au	*aw, o*	ka**u**nti'	"ka*w*nti', k**o**nti'"	*a little*
ay	*ey, e*	m**ay**	"m*ey*, m**e**"	*there's (a/some)...*
diy, dy	*j*	d**iy**an, d**y**aryo	"*j*an," "*j*aryo"	*there, newspaper*
niy	*ñ (ny)*	n**iy**og	"*ñ*og (*ny*og)"	*coconut*
siy, sy	*sh*	s**iy**a, mas**y**ado	"*sh*a," "ma*sh*ado"	*he/she, too (much)*
tiy, ty	*ch*	t**iy**ak, t**y**an	"*ch*ak," "*ch*an"	*doubtless, belly*
ts	*ch*	ko**ts**e, **ts**okol**a**te	"ko*ch*e, "cho*k*ol**a**te"	*car, chocolate*

Forming and connecting words

Roots and affixes

The building blocks of Tagalog words are roots and affixes. Roots can stand on their own while affixes cannot. In words comprising of a root and one or more affixes, the root carries the core meaning of the word.

Example in English: In the word *uneventful, event* is the root while *un-* and *-ful* are affixes.

Examples of Tagalog roots:

anak	*child (son or daughter)*
araw	*day, sun*
gabi	*night, evening*

Some roots can be repeated to form a new word.

| araw-araw | *every day* |
| gabi-gabi | *every night* |

Some roots can be combined to form a new word.

araw-gabi	*day and night*
anak-araw	*albino*

Finally, various affixes can be added at the beginning, in the middle and/or at the end of a root.

*ma*araw	*sunny*
tag-araw	*summer*
*ka*arawa*n*	*birthday*
*ka*gabi	*last night*
gu*m*abi	*to be or become evening*

Sound changes when combining roots and affixes

In some cases, a sound change occurs when a root and an affix are combined. Such changes are reflected in the spelling. Examples:

sound change	root	affix	root + affix
from /d/ to /r/	_d_unong _knowledge_ **tawi_d_** _crossing_	ma- -in	ma_r_unong _to know how_ tawi_r_in _to cross_
from /o/ to /u/	**put_o_l** _cut off_	-in	put_u_lin _to cut off_
from /ng/ to /n/*	dikit _sticking_ **_l_uto'** _cooking_	pa_ng_-	pa_n_dikit _paste, glue_ pa_n_**_l_uto'** _cooking utensil_
from /ng/ to /m/**	bansa' _nation_ **pito** _seven_	pa_ng_-	pa_m_bansa' _national_ pa_m_pito _seventh_

* usually before **d, l, r, s, t,** and sometimes before **n**
** usually before **b, p,** and sometimes before **m**

In some cases, the final vowel or the first consonant of the root
disappears. Examples:

root	affix	root + affix
taki**p** *cover, lid*	-an	takpan *to cover*
sunod *next, following*	-in	sundin *to obey*
kuha' *getting*	mang-	manguha' *to collect or gather*

In the case of the affixes **-in** and **-an**, /h/ or /n/ is added when the root
ends in a vowel that is not followed by a glottal stop. Examples:

root	affix	root + affix
kati *itch*	-in	katihin *to feel itchy*
talo *defeated, beaten*	-in	talunin *to defeat, to beat*
mura *cheap*	-an	murahan *to reduce the price of, to make cheaper*
tawa *laughter*	-an	tawanan *to laugh at*

Syllable repetition

Syllable repetition is common in Tagalog. There are two types:

1. The first syllable is repeated (rep1).

If the syllable starts with a vowel, repeat the first vowel. Example:

alis	_a_**alis**
departure	_will leave_

If the syllable starts with a consonant, repeat the first consonant and the first vowel. Examples:

basa	_ba_**ba**sa
reading	_will read_
prito	mag_pi_**pri**to*
fried	_will fry_

* **mag-** is an affix.

2. The first two syllables are repeated (rep2). A hyphen is generally added. Example:

dalawa	_dala_-**dalawa**
two	_in twos, in pairs_

Na/-ng

Na/-ng is used to link certain words together. For instance, it is used to link adjectives with what they are describing.

na/-ng	rule: use after words ending in—	example	
na	a consonant other than /n/	**mabait *na* ba<u>bae</u>**	*nice woman*
-ng	a vowel or /n/*	**maganda*ng* ba<u>bae</u>** **ma<u>ya</u>mang ba<u>bae</u>**	*pretty woman* *rich woman*

* /**ng**/ replaces /**n**/.

Na/-ng can also be understood as *that, which* or *who*. Examples:

<u>a</u>so*ng* tumalon	*dog **that** jumped*
<u>ba</u>ta*ng* kumanta	*child **that** sang*
ballpe*ng* na<u>hu</u>log ballpen *na* na<u>hu</u>log*	*pen **that** fell*

* When used to mean *that, which* or *who,* **na** may also be used after words ending in a vowel or /**n**/.

Other uses of **na/-ng** are covered in later chapters.

Basic word order

The POD and the News

Basic sentences generally have two parts—the Point of Departure and the News.

The POD

The Point of Departure (POD) is the starting point of a basic sentence. It is the object, person, idea etc. that the speaker thinks about before or as he or she begins the sentence.

The POD is picked by the speaker from among the things that he or she assumes the listener knows. Generally, things assumed to be known to the listener are those that—

- have been previously mentioned or implied,
- are in sight or in the situation, and/or
- are shared or common (general) knowledge.

Examples:

Ma<u>ha</u>ba' *ang email.*	*The email is long.*
Puti' *ang dingding.*	*The wall is white.*

Bilog *ang mundo*.	*The world is round.*
Mammal *ang balyena*.	*Whales (in general) are mammals.*
Italyano *si Da Vinci*.	*Da Vinci was Italian.*

| <u>Pin</u>san ni Mary *si John*. | *John is Mary's cousin.* |
| <u>Pin</u>san ni John *si Mary*. | *Mary is John's cousin.* |

* Even though these sentences mean the same thing, their PODs are different.

The News

The News is what is said about the POD. It is the relatively new information communicated to the listener.

In basic Tagalog sentences, the News generally comes before the POD. Examples:

News	POD	Translation
Teacher *teacher*	**ang ba<u>bae</u>.** *the woman*	*The woman is a teacher.*
Ku<u>main</u> *ate*	**ang ba<u>bae</u>.** *the woman*	*The woman ate.*
Ku<u>main</u> ng ice cream *ate ice cream*	**ang ba<u>bae</u>.** *the woman*	*The woman ate ice cream.*
Maganda *pretty*	**ang ba<u>bae</u>.** *the woman*	*The woman is pretty.*

Nasa school *in school*	**ang babae.** *the woman*	*The woman is in school.*
May kotse *has a car*	**ang babae.** *the woman*	*The woman has a car.*

In conversation, the POD can be omitted when it has just been mentioned. For example, the question, *"Who is John?"* can be answered in Tagalog with—

Pinsan ni Mary.	*Mary's cousin.*

While the question, *"What did the dog do?"* can be answered with—

Kumain. Tapos natulog.	*Ate. Then slept.*

Note:

1. In certain sentences, the POD comes before the News. See also: POD-first sentences (p. 424)

2. Various other terms have been used to refer to the POD and the News. See also: Appendix B: Terminology (p. 445)

The Tagalog POD and the English subject

In many cases, the Tagalog POD corresponds to the English subject. Examples:

Ku<u>ma</u>in ng ice cream si Mary.	*Mary ate ice cream.*
Pumunta sa teacher si Mary.	*Mary went to the teacher.*

However, there are also many cases in which the Tagalog POD does not correspond to the English subject. Examples:

Ki<u>na</u>in ni Mary ang ice cream.	*Mary ate the ice cream.* Lit. *The ice cream was eaten by Mary.*
Pinuntahan ni Mary ang teacher.	*Mary went to the teacher.* Lit. *The teacher was gone to by Mary.*

Some of the main differences between the Tagalog POD and the English subject:

1. The Tagalog POD generally comes after the News. The English subject comes before the predicate.

Ku<u>ma</u>in ng ice cream si Mary.	*Mary ate ice cream.*
Pumunta sa teacher si Mary.	*Mary went to the teacher.*

2. The English subject is usually the doer or "experiencer"* of the action. The Tagalog POD may be the doer/experiencer, object, direction etc. of the action.

Kumain ng ice cream *si Mary.* (POD – doer)	*Mary ate ice cream.*
Kinain ni Mary *ang ice cream.* (POD – object)	*Mary ate **the ice cream.*** Lit. ***The ice cream** was eaten by Mary.*

Pumunta sa teacher *si Mary.* (POD – doer)	*Mary went to the teacher.*
Pinuntahan ni Mary *ang teacher.* (POD – direction)	*Mary went to **the teacher.*** Lit. ***The teacher** was gone to by Mary.*

* Example of a Tagalog POD and English subject as experiencer of the action:

Nagulat *si Mary.*	*Mary was startled.*

3. The Tagalog POD is usually either definite (e.g. the dog, your dog, that dog, John) or generic (e.g. dogs in general).

Pinsan ni Mary *si John.*	*John is Mary's cousin.*
Mammal *ang balyena.*	***Whales** (in general) are mammals.*
Masarap *ang ice cream.*	***The ice cream** is delicious.* ***Ice cream** (in general) is delicious.*

It is not uncommon for an English subject to be indefinite (e.g. a dog, some dogs).

A bridge will be built here.
A wallet has been found.

The Tagalog equivalent is generally expressed using a POD-less sentence indicating existence *(There's a…).*

May tulay na itatayo' dito.	*A bridge will be built here.* Lit. *There's a bridge that will be built here.*
May wallet na nahanap.	*A wallet has been found.* Lit. *There's a wallet that has been found.*

See also: Sentences with no POD (p. 421), **May, mayroon/meron, marami, wala'** (p. 379)

4. If the object of an action in a basic sentence is definite, it becomes the POD in Tagalog. But it does not have to be the subject in English.

Kumain ng ice cream *si Mary.*	*Mary ate (some) ice cream.* (ice cream – indefinite object)
Kinain ni Mary *ang ice cream.*	*Mary ate the ice cream.* Lit. *The ice cream was eaten by Mary.* (the ice cream – definite object)

5. Certain other English subjects have no equivalent Tagalog POD.

Umuulan.	*It's raining.* Lit. *Raining.*

Markers

Markers are short words that indicate the role of a word in a sentence. There are three groups of markers—the Ang, Ng and Sa markers.

Ang markers

The Ang markers are **si, ang, sina** and **ang mga**.

singular	for personal names	si
	for all others	ang (yung)
plural	for personal names	sina
	for all others	ang mga (yung mga)

Note:

1. **mga** is pronounced as *"manga."*

2. Personal names are names that refer to specific persons, animals, cartoon characters or anything with a personality.

3. **Yung** is often used in conversation. **Iyong** is also sometimes used as an alternative to **ang**.

Examples:

ang ba<u>bae</u>	*the woman* *women (in general)*
ang mga ba<u>bae</u>	*the women*
ang <u>a</u>so	*the dog* *dogs (in general)*
ang mga <u>a</u>so	*the dogs*

si Alfred	*Alfred*
sina Alfred	*Alfred and company*
sina Alfred at Mary	*Alfred and Mary*
si Donald Duck	*Donald Duck*
sina Donald Duck	*Donald Duck and company*

ang World Cup	*the World Cup*
ang Japan	*Japan*
ang mga Toyota	*the Toyotas*

sina Mr. Brown	*Mr. Brown and company*
ang mga Brown	*the Browns*

si Mary	*(the person) Mary*
Mary	*(the name) Mary*

Uses of Ang markers

1. Marking the POD (p. 35) of a sentence.

Teacher *ang ba<u>ba</u>e.*	*The woman is a teacher.*
Ku<u>ma</u>in *ang ba<u>ba</u>e.*	*The woman ate.*

2. Marking the News, if it refers to a particular person or thing.

Ang teacher ang ba<u>ba</u>e.	*The woman is the teacher.*
Si Mary ang ba<u>ba</u>e.	*The woman is Mary.*

Ng markers

The Ng markers are **ni, ng, nina** and **ng mga**.

singular	for personal names	**ni**
	for all others	**ng** **(nung)**
plural	for personal names	**nina**
	for all others	**ng mga** **(nung mga)**

Note:

1. **ng** is pronounced as *"nang."*

2. **mga** is pronounced as *"manga."*

3. Personal names are names that refer to specific persons, animals, cartoon characters or anything with a personality.

4. **Nung** is often used in conversation. **Niyong** and **nyung** are also sometimes used as alternatives to **ng**.

Common uses of Ng markers

1. Showing possession or belonging *("of")*.

bag ng ba<u>bae</u>	*a/the woman's bag* Lit. *bag of a/the woman*
bag ni Mary	*Mary's bag* Lit. *bag of Mary*
apartment nina Alfred at Mary	*Alfred and Mary's apartment* Lit. *apartment of Alfred and Mary*
bubong ng <u>ba</u>hay	*roof of a/the house*
presi<u>den</u>te ng Pili<u>pi</u>nas	*president of the Philippines*

2. Expressing various kinds of specification *("of")*.

<u>gru</u>po ng ba<u>bae</u>	*group of women*
<u>bo</u>te ng beer	*bottle of beer*

picture ng <u>a</u>so	*picture of a/the dog*
teacher ng Math	*teacher of Math*
manla<u>la</u>ro' ng basketball	*basketball player* Lit. *player of basketball*
tam<u>ba</u>kan ng ba<u>su</u>ra	*garbage dump* Lit. *dumping place of garbage*
isang <u>ki</u>lo ng mangga	*a kilo of mangoes*

3. Only for **ng** and **ng mga**: Marking the non-POD object of an action. A non-POD object is an object that is part of the News (p. 35) instead of the POD (p. 35). The non-POD object is often indefinite (*"a/an/some"* + noun).

Ku<u>ma</u>in* *ng mangga* ang ba<u>ba</u>e.	*The woman ate* **a mango.** *The woman ate* **some mangoes.**
Ku<u>ma</u>in *ng ice cream* ang ba<u>ba</u>e.	*The woman ate* **(some)** *ice cream.*

4. Marking the non-POD doer of an action *("by")*. A non-POD doer is a doer that is part of the News (p. 35) instead of the POD (p. 35). In most cases, the non-POD doer is definite *("the"* + noun).

Ki<u>na</u>in* *ng ba<u>ba</u>e* ang ice cream.	*The woman ate the ice cream.* Lit. *The ice cream was eaten by the woman.*
Ki<u>na</u>in *ni Mary* ang ice cream.	*Mary ate the ice cream.* Lit. *The ice cream was eaten by Mary.*

* The difference between ki<u>na</u>in and ku<u>ma</u>in is explained in the chapter on verbs (p. 105).

To make the non-POD doer unambiguously indefinite, **isang** may be added.

Ki<u>na</u>in *ng isang ba<u>ba</u>e* ang ice cream.	*A woman ate the ice cream.* Lit. *The ice cream was eaten by a woman.*

5. Only for **ng**: Indicating direction. In some cases, **ng** may be used to indicate direction. This direction should be a place (not a movable object or person). Examples:

Pumunta *ng school* ang ba<u>ba</u>e.	*The woman went to school.*
Pumunta *ng Pili<u>pi</u>nas* ang ba<u>ba</u>e.	*The woman went to the Philippines.*
Umakyat *ng bundok* ang ba<u>ba</u>e.	*The woman climbed a mountain.*

Sa markers

The Sa markers are **kay, sa, kina** and **sa mga.**

singular	for personal names	**kay**
	for all others	**sa**
plural	for personal names	**kina**
	for all others	**sa mga**

Note:

1. **mga** is pronounced as *"manga."*

2. Personal names are names that refer to specific persons, animals, cartoon characters or anything with a personality.

Common uses of Sa markers

1. Showing possession or belonging *("'s")*.

Kay Ralph **ang bag.**	*The bag is **Ralph's**.*
Sa <u>*ba*</u>*ta'* **ang bag.**	*The bag **belongs to the child**.* Lit. *The bag is **the child's**.*

2. Indicating location or direction *("in, on, at, into, onto, to, towards, from, through etc.")*.

Ku<u>ma</u>in *sa school* ang ba<u>bae</u>.	*The woman ate **at school.***
Pumunta *sa school* ang ba<u>bae</u>.	*The woman went **to school.***

Note: In some cases, **ng** may also be used to indicate direction (p. 48).

3. Marking the non-POD "direction" of an action. The direction of an action is the person or thing, for which or in whose direction the action is performed. A non-POD direction is a direction that is part of the News (p. 35) instead of the POD (p. 35). The non-POD direction may be definite or indefinite.

Su<u>mu</u>lat *kay Mary* ang ba<u>bae</u>.	*The woman wrote **(to) Mary.***
Nagtanong *sa doktor* ang ba<u>bae</u>.	*The woman asked **a/the doctor.***

Difference between direction and object:

direction of an action	object of an action
*write **(to) Mary**, write **(to) me***	*write **a letter**, write **a list***
*ask **the docter**, ask **her***	*ask **a question**, ask **his name***

Summary

		Ang	Ng	Sa
singular	for personal names	si	ni	kay
	for all others	ang (yung)	ng (nung)	sa
plural	for personal names	sina	nina	kina
	for all others	ang mga (yung mga)	ng mga (nung mga)	sa mga

Pronouns

Pronouns can be divided into the same three groups that are used to classify markers (p. 43). Ang, Ng and Sa pronouns generally have the same roles in a sentence as phrases introduced by an Ang, Ng or Sa marker, respectively.

Ang pronouns

Personal pronouns

pronoun	translation
ako	*I*
ikaw, ka	*you (singular)*
siya	*he/she*
kami	*we (excluding you)*
tayo	*we (including you)*
kayo	*you (plural)*
sila	*they*

Ikaw and ka

Ikaw and **ka** both mean *you*. **Ikaw** is used in the News (p. 35) of a sentence, while **ka** is used in the POD (p. 35). Examples:

Ikaw ang pa<u>na</u>lo.	*The winner is you.*
Maganda *ka*.	*You are pretty.*

Exception: **Ikaw** is used in the POD in POD-first sentences (p. 424), which are less common in everyday speech.

Kami and <u>ta</u>yo

kami	*we (excluding the listener)*
<u>ta</u>yo	*we (including the listener)*

Examples:

Teacher *kami*.	*We (e.g. my wife and I) are teachers.*
Teacher *<u>ta</u>yo*.	*We (e.g. you, my wife and I) are teachers.* *We (e.g. you and I) are teachers.*

Polite "you"

Kayo, *you (plural)*, is used instead of **ikaw/ka**, *you (singular)*, to address older people, superiors, adult strangers and adult customers.

Sila, *they*, is also often used to address customers and high-ranking officials. It is also used when asking an adult stranger who he or she is. Example:

Sino po' sila?	*May I have your name, please?*
	May I know who you are?
	Who's speaking?
	Lit. *Who are they?*

See also: **po'/ho'** [1] (p. 369)

Demonstrative pronouns

pronoun	translation
ito	*this (near me)*
iyan	*that (near you)*
iyon	*that/it (far from you and me)*
ang mga ito **itong mga ito**	*these (near me)*
ang mga iyan **iyang mga iyan**	*those (near you)*
ang mga iyon **iyong mga iyon**	*those/they (far from you and me)*

Clarification: near me etc.

near me	the thing or idea is closer to or more closely identified with the speaker
near you	the thing or idea is closer to or more closely identified with the listener(s)
far from you and me	the thing or idea is neither close to nor closely identified with the speaker or the listener(s)

This dog, that dog etc.

pronoun	translation
ang asong ito itong asong ito	*this dog (near me)*
ang asong iyan iyang asong iyan	*that dog (near you)*
ang asong iyon iyong asong iyon	*that dog (far from you and me)*
ang mga asong ito itong mga asong ito	*these dogs (near me)*
ang mga asong iyan iyang mga asong iyan	*those dogs (near you)*
ang mga asong iyon iyong mga asong iyon	*those dogs (far from you and me)*

Note:

1. **Na/-ng** (p. 34) is used to link **ito/iyan/iyon** with the noun.

2. The second **ito/iyan/iyon** may be dropped when more information about the noun is given right after it. Example:

ito**ng** **a**so**ng** malaki at mabait	*this big and friendly dog*

Shortened forms

Ito, iyan and **iyon** are often shortened to **'to, 'yan** and **'yon/'yun** in spoken Tagalog.

Uses of Ang pronouns

1. Constituting the POD (p. 35) of a sentence.

Teacher *siya*.	*He/she is a teacher.*
Kumain *siya*.	*He/she ate.*
Bago *ito*.	*This is new.*

2. Constituting the News (p. 35).

Siya **ang mayor.**	*He/she's the mayor.* Lit. *The mayor is* **he/she.**
Ito **ang dahilan.**	*This is the reason.* Lit. *The reason is* **this.**

See also: Uses of Ang markers (p. 45)

Ng pronouns

Personal pronouns

pronoun	literal translations
ko	*my, (by) me*
mo	*your, (by) you (singular)*
niya	*his/her, (by) him/her*
namin	*our, (by) us (excluding you)*
natin	*our, (by) us (including you)*
ninyo / niyo	*your, (by) you (plural)*
nila	*their, (by) them*

For example sentences, see Common uses of Ng pronouns (p. 61).

Namin and natin

namin	*our, (by) us (excluding the listener)*
natin	*our, (by) us (including the listener)*

See also: **Kami** and **tayo** (p. 54)

Polite "your, (by) you"

Ninyo / **niyo**, *your, (by) you (plural)*, and **nila**, *their, (by) them*, are used as the polite alternatives to **mo**, *your, (by) you (singular)*.

See also: Polite "you" (p. 54)

Demonstrative pronouns

pronoun	literal translations
nito	*(of/by) this (near me)*
niyan	*(of/by) that (near you)*
niyon / noon	*(of/by) that/it (far from you and me)*
ng mga ito **nitong mga ito**	*(of/by) these (near me)*
ng mga iyan **niyang mga iyan**	*(of/by) those (near you)*
ng mga iyon **niyong / noong mga iyon**	*(of/by) those/them (far from you and me)*

For example sentences, see Common uses of Ng pronouns (p. 61).

See also: Clarification: near me etc. (p. 56)

This dog, that dog etc.

pronoun	literal translations
ng a̲so̱ng ito **nito̱ng a̲so̱ng ito**	*(of/by) this dog (near me)*
ng a̲so̱ng iyan **niyang a̲so̱ng iyan**	*(of/by) that dog (near you)*
ng a̲so̱ng iyon **noong a̲so̱ng iyon**	*(of/by) that dog (far from you and me)*
ng mga a̲so̱ng ito **nito̱ng mga a̲so̱ng ito**	*(of/by) these dogs (near me)*
ng mga a̲so̱ng iyan **niyang mga a̲so̱ng iyan**	*(of/by) those dogs (near you)*
ng mga a̲so̱ng iyon **noong mga a̲so̱ng iyon**	*(of/by) those dogs (far from you and me)*

Note:

1. **Na/-ng** (p. 34) is used to link **nito/niyan/niyon/noon** and **ito/iyan/iyon** with the noun.

2. In phrases using **nito/niyan/niyon/noon**, the final **ito/iyan/iyon** may be dropped when more information about the noun is given right after it. Example:

nito̱ng a̲so̱ng malaki at mabait	*(of/by) this big and friendly dog*

Shortened forms

In spoken Tagalog—

*   **noong** is often shortened to **nung**
*   **ito, iyan** and **iyon** are often shortened to **'to, 'yan** and **'yon/'yun**

Common uses of Ng pronouns

1. Showing possession or belonging.

bag *niya*	*his/her bag*
bag *ko*	*my bag*
re<u>sul</u>ta *nito*	*result of this*
picture *ng <u>a</u>song ito*	*picture of this dog*

2. Only for demonstrative pronouns: Marking the non-POD object of an action. A non-POD object is an object that is part of the News (p. 35) instead of the POD (p. 35). The non-POD object is often indefinite (*"some of this/that"*).

Ku<u>ma</u>in* *nito* **ang** ba<u>ba</u>e.	*The woman ate some of this.*

3. Marking the non-POD doer of an action *("by")*. A non-POD doer is a doer that is part of the News (p. 35) instead of the POD (p. 35).

Ki<u>na</u>in* *niya* **ang ice cream.**	*He/she ate the ice cream.* Lit. *The ice cream was eaten **by** him/her.*
Ki<u>na</u>in *ko* **ang ice cream.**	*I ate the ice cream.* Lit. *The ice cream was eaten **by** me.*
Ki<u>na</u>in *nito* **ang ice cream.**	*This (person/animal) ate the ice cream.* Lit. *The ice cream was eaten **by** this.*
Ki<u>na</u>in *ng <u>a</u>song ito* **ang ice cream.**	*This dog ate the ice cream.* Lit. *The ice cream was eaten **by** this dog.*

* The difference between **ki<u>na</u>in** and **ku<u>ma</u>in** is explained in the chapter on verbs (p. 105).

See also: Common uses of Ng markers (p. 46)

Sa pronouns

Personal pronouns

pronoun	literal translations
(sa) akin	*mine, (to etc.) me*
(sa) iyo	*yours, (to etc.) you (singular)*
(sa) kanya	*his/hers, (to etc.) him/her*
(sa) amin	*ours, (to etc.) us (excluding you)*
(sa) atin	*ours, (to etc.) us (including you)*
(sa) inyo	*yours, (to etc.) you (plural)*
(sa) kanila	*theirs, (to etc.) them*

For example sentences, see Common uses of Sa pronouns (p. 66).

(Sa) amin and (sa) atin

(sa) amin	*ours, (to etc.) us (excluding the listener)*
(sa) atin	*ours, (to etc.) us (including the listener)*

See also: **Kami** and **tayo** (p. 54)

Polite "yours, (to etc.) you"

(Sa) inyo, *yours, (to etc.) you (plural)*, and **(sa) kanila**, *theirs, (to etc.) them*, are used as the polite alternatives to **(sa) iyo**, *yours, (to etc.) you (singular)*.

See also: Polite "you" (p. 54)

Demonstrative pronouns

pronoun	literal translations
<u>di</u>to / <u>ri</u>to	*(to etc.) this, here (near me)*
diyan / riyan	*(to etc.) that, there (near you)*
doon / roon	*(to etc.) that/it, over there (far from you and me)*
sa mga ito	*(to etc.) these (near me)*
sa mga iyan	*(to etc.) those (near you)*
sa mga iyon	*(to etc.) those/them (far from you and me)*

For example sentences, see Common uses of Sa pronouns (p. 66).

See also: Clarification: near me etc. (p. 56)

This dog, that dog etc.

pronoun	literal translations
sa asong ito dito sa asong ito	(to etc.) this dog (near me)
sa asong iyan diyan sa asong iyan	(to etc.) that dog (near you)
sa asong iyon doon sa asong iyon	(to etc.) that dog (far from you and me)
sa mga asong ito dito sa mga asong ito	(to etc.) these dogs (near me)
sa mga asong iyan diyan sa mga asong iyan	(to etc.) those dogs (near you)
sa mga asong iyon doon sa mga asong iyon	(to etc.) those dogs (far from you and me)

Note:

1. Sa and na/-ng (p. 34) are used to link dito/diyan/doon and ito/iyan/iyon, respectively, with the noun.

2. In phrases using dito/diyan/doon, the final ito/iyan/iyon may be dropped when more information about the noun is given right after it. Example:

dito sa asong malaki at mabait	(to etc.) this big and friendly dog

Shortened forms

In spoken Tagalog—

- **doon** and **roon** are often shortened to **don/dun** and **ron**
- **ito, iyan** and **iyon** are often shortened to **'to, 'yan** and **'yon/'yun**

Common uses of Sa pronouns

1. Only for personal pronouns and some demonstrative pronouns:
Showing possession or belonging.

Sa kanya ang bag. *Kanya* ang bag.	*The bag is **his/hers**.*
<u>A</u>kin ang bag.	*The bag is **mine**.*
Sa <u>a</u>song ito ang <u>ku</u>mot.	*The blanket **belongs to this dog**.* Lit. *The blanket is **this dog's**.*

"Sa pronoun + **-ng**" can be used as a formal alternative to a Ng pronoun
showing possession (p. 61).

bag *niya* *kanyang* **bag**	*his/her bag (formal)*
bag *ko* <u>a</u>*king* **bag**	*my bag (formal)*

2. Indicating location or direction.

Ku*main* **doon** ang ba**bae**.	*The woman ate* **there**.
Pumunta **doon** ang ba**bae**.	*The woman went* **there**.
Pumunta *sa kanya* ang ba**bae**.	*The woman went* **to** *him/her*.
Pumunta *sa asong iyon* ang ba**bae**.	*The woman went* **to that dog** *(far from you and me)*.

3. Marking the non-POD direction of an action. The direction of an action is the person or thing, for which or in whose direction the action is performed. A non-POD direction is a direction that is part of the News (p. 35) instead of the POD (p. 35).

Su*mulat sa kanya* ang ba**bae**.	*The woman wrote* **(to)** *him/her*.
Nagtanong *sa kanya* ang ba**bae**.	*The woman asked* **him/her**.
Nagtanong *sa mga iyon* ang ba**bae**.	*The woman asked* **those** *(people) / them*.

See also:

- Difference between direction and object (p. 50)
- Common uses of Sa markers (p. 49)

Summary: markers and pronouns

		Ang	Ng	Sa
singular	for personal names	si	ni	kay
	for all others	ang (yung)	ng (nung)	sa
plural	for personal names	sina	nina	kina
	for all others	ang mga (yung mga)	ng mga (nung mga)	sa mga

	Ang	Ng	Sa
I, my etc.	ako	ko	(sa) akin
you, your etc. (singular)	ikaw, ka	mo	(sa) iyo
he/she, his/her etc.	siya	niya	(sa) kanya
we, our etc. (excluding you)	kami	namin	(sa) amin
we, our etc. (including you)	tayo	natin	(sa) atin
you, your etc. (plural)	kayo	ninyo / niyo	(sa) inyo
they, their etc.	sila	nila	(sa) kanila

this etc. (near me)	ito	nito	<u>di</u>to / <u>ri</u>to
that etc. (near you)	iyan	niyan	diyan / riyan
that/it etc. (far from you and me)	iyon	niyon / noon	doon / roon
these etc. (near me)	ang mga ito itong mga ito	ng mga ito nitong mga ito	sa mga ito
those etc. (near you)	ang mga iyan iyang mga iyan	ng mga iyan niyang mga iyan	sa mga iyan
those/they etc. (far from you and me)	ang mga iyon iyong mga iyon	ng mga iyon niyong / noong mga iyon	sa mga iyon

In this book, Ang phrase, Ng phrase and Sa phrase are used to refer to the three marker and pronoun groups.

phrase	refers to—	examples
Ang phrase	• phrases introduced by an Ang marker, • Ang pronouns	ang ba<u>bae</u> si Bill siya ito
Ng phrase	• phrases introduced by a Ng marker, • Ng pronouns	ng ba<u>bae</u> ni Bill niya nito
Sa phrase	• phrases introduced by a Sa marker, • Sa pronouns	sa ba<u>bae</u> kay Bill kanya <u>di</u>to

See also:

- Ang markers (p. 43), Ang pronouns (p. 53)
- Ng markers (p. 45), Ng pronouns (p. 58)
- Sa markers (p. 49), Sa pronouns (p. 63)

Kita

When—

- the speaker is the non-POD doer (p. 62) of the action **(ko)**, and
- the listener is the POD (p. 35) and the object of the action **(ka)**,

the combination **ko–ka** (*I* as doer–*you* as object) is replaced by **kita**.

Examples:

Na<u>ki</u>ta' *kita*.	*I saw you.* Lit. *You were seen by me.*
Mahal *kita*.	*I love you.* Lit. *You are loved by me.*

Compare with:

Na<u>ki</u>ta' *ko si Fred*.	*I saw Fred.* Lit. *Fred was seen by me.*
Na<u>ki</u>ta' *ko siya*.	*I saw him/her.* Lit. *He/she was seen by me.*
Mahal *ko si Fred*.	*I love Fred.* Lit. *Fred is loved by me.*
Mahal *ko siya*.	*I love him/her.* Lit. *He/she is loved by me.*

Kami ni John etc.

"Plural personal pronoun + Ng phrase" is generally understood as follows:

kami	*we (excluding you)*
kami ni John	*John and I*
kami nina John	*John and others and I*
kami nina John at Mark	*John, Mark and I*
kami ng babae	*the woman and I*
kami ng mga babae	*the women and I/us*

tayo	*we (including you)*
tayo ni John	*John, you and I*
tayo nina John	*John and others, you and I*
tayo nina John at Mark	*John, Mark, you and I*
tayo ng babae	*the woman, you and I*
tayo ng mga babae	*the women, you and I/us*

kayo	*you (plural)*
kayo ni John	*John and you (singular)*
kayo nina John	*John and others and you (sg.)*
kayo nina John at Mark	*John, Mark and you (sg.)*

kayo ng ba<u>bae</u>	*the woman and you (sg.)*
kayo ng mga ba<u>bae</u>	*the women and you (sg./pl.)*

sila	*they*
sila ni John	*he/she and John*
sila nina John	*he/she, John and others*
sila nina John at Mark	*he/she, John and Mark*
sila ng ba<u>bae</u>	*he/she and the woman*
sila ng mga ba<u>bae</u>	*he/she/they and the women*

Sentences:

Ku<u>ma</u>in *kami ni John.*	*John and I ate.*
Ku<u>ma</u>in *kami nina John at* Mark.	*John, Mark and I ate.*

Ku<u>ma</u>in *sila ni John.*	*He/she and John ate.*
Ki<u>na</u>in *nila ni John* ang mangga.	*He/she and John ate the mango.* Lit. *The mango was eaten by him/her and John.*
Su<u>mu</u>lat *sa kanila ni John* ang ba<u>bae</u>.	*The woman wrote (to) him/her and John.*

See also:

- Ang personal pronouns (p. 53)
- Ng personal pronouns (p. 58)
- Sa personal pronouns (p. 63)
- **Kami** and <u>tayo</u> (p. 54)
- Ng markers (p. 45)

Mismo

ako <u>mis</u>mo	*I myself*
si John <u>mis</u>mo	*John himself*
ang ba<u>bae</u> <u>mis</u>mo	*the woman herself*

Sentences:

Pumunta *ako* <u>*mis*</u>*mo*.	*I myself went.*
Pumunta *si John* <u>*mis*</u>*mo*.	*John himself went.*

When used in the News (p. 35) of a sentence, <u>**mismo**</u> can also come before the noun or the pronoun. **Na/-ng** (p. 34) is added in this case. Examples:

Ako <u>*mis*</u>*mo* **ang pumunta.*** <u>*Mis*</u>*mong ako* **ang pumunta.**	*The one who went was **I** **myself**.*
Si John <u>*mis*</u>*mo* **ang pumunta.** <u>*Mis*</u>*mong si John* **ang pumunta.**	*The one who went was **John** **himself**.*

* See also: Verbs, adjectives etc. used as nouns (p. 101)

Note: **Mismo** can also be used to add emphasis to a word or a phrase (*"right"* or *"very"*).

sa gitna' _mismo_	*right in the middle*
dito _mismo_	*right here*
sa sunod na _araw_ _mismo_	*the very next day*

Nouns

Gender

A few nouns have a female equivalent that ends in /a/. Examples:

male	female	translation
Pilipino	Pilipina	*Filipino*
doktor	doktora	*doctor*
tindero	tindera	*vendor, shopkeeper*
Amerikano	Amerikana	*American*
propesor	propesora	*professor*
Italyano	Italyana	*Italian*
Mexicano	Mexicana	*Mexican*

Plurals

Noun plurals are formed by placing **mga** *("manga")* before the noun. Examples:

kapatid	*sibling*
mga kapatid	*siblings*

Below are other ways to indicate the plural number:

1. Using numbers or other words expressing quantity. See also: Expressing quantity or distribution (p. 269), **Na/-ng** (p. 34)

isang kapatid	*one sibling*
dalawang kapatid	*two siblings*
tatlong kapatid	*three siblings*
maraming kapatid	*many siblings*

2. Using plural adjectives. See also: Plural adjectives (p. 262), **Na/-ng** (p. 34)

masipag na kapatid	*diligent sibling*
masisipag na kapatid	*diligent siblings*
napakasipag na kapatid	*very diligent sibling*
napakasisipag na kapatid	*very diligent siblings*

3. Using affixes expressing or describing two or more persons or things. See also: noun affixes **mag-** (p. 86) and **mag-** +rep1 [1] (p. 88), and adjective affixes **magka-** (p. 247) and **magkaka-** (p. 248)

kapatid	*sibling*
*ma*gkapatid	*two persons who are siblings*
*magka*kapatid	*three or more persons who are siblings*

Optionally, the plural number can be indicated by combining **mga** with a number, any other word expressing quantity, or a plural adjective.

ma<u>ra</u>ming kapatid	*many siblings*
ma<u>ra</u>ming *mga* kapatid	*many siblings*
masi<u>si</u>pag na kapatid	*diligent siblings*
mga masi<u>si</u>pag na kapatid	*diligent siblings*

Note:

1. If the News (p. 35) of the sentence is a number, **mga** cannot be used in the POD (p. 35). Example:

Lima ang anak niya.*	*He/she has five children.*
	Lit. *His/her children are five.*

* **Mga** cannot be placed before **anak**.

2. **Mga** means *about* or *around* when used before a number or a time expression. Examples:

mga limang kilo	*about 5 kilos*
mga 1 o'clock	*at around 1 o'clock*

Noun affixes

The most common noun affixes are given below, together with a number of examples.

The roots and root-affix combinations may have more meanings than the ones given here.

See also:

- Roots and affixes (p. 29)
- Sound changes when combining roots and affixes (p. 31)
- Syllable repetition (p. 33)

-an [1]

a place where a large quantity of the thing meant by the root is put, planted, or can be found

root	meaning	root + affix	meaning
ba**su**ra	*garbage*	**ba**surahan	*trash can, rubbish bin*
aklat	*book*	ak**la**tan	*library*

damo	grass	damuhan	lawn, meadow
palay	rice plant, unhusked rice	palayan	rice field, rice paddy

-an [2]

a place where the action expressed by the root is performed

root	meaning	root + affix	meaning
kain	eating	kainan	a place where people eat (e.g. a restaurant, café, cafeteria)

-an [3]

a period in which the action expressed by the root is collectively performed

root	meaning	root + affix	meaning
ani	harvest	anihan	harvest time
pasok	entry, class, work	pasukan	school period, school year

-an [4]

a tool or an object that is used to measure what is meant by the root

root	meaning	root + affix	meaning
oras	*time*	orasan	*clock, watch*
timbang	*weight*	timbangan	*weighing scale*

-an [5]

reciprocal or joint performance of the action expressed by the root

root	meaning	root + affix	meaning
sayaw	*dance, dancing*	sayawan	*dancing together (e.g. a ball)*
kanta	*song, singing*	kantahan	*singing together (e.g. a karaoke party)*
saksak	*stab, stabbing*	saksakan	*stabbing one another*
kain	*eating*	kainan	*eating together, a feast*

-in

an object of the action expressed by the root

root	meaning	root + affix	meaning
awit	*song, singing*	awitin	*song*
bili	*buying, buying price*	bilihin	*something to buy, goods*
aral	*lesson, studying*	aralin	*studies*

ka-

a person or a thing with whom the place, object, quality or situation expressed by the root is shared

root	meaning	root + affix	meaning
klase	*class*	kaklase	*classmate*
opisina	*office*	kaopisina	*colleague, co-worker*
usap	*talking*	kausap	*someone being talked to (a conversation "partner")*
tumbas	*value*	katumbas	*something of equal value*
tabi	*side*	katabi	*someone/something beside someone/something else*

ka- +rep1, kaka-

the act of doing the action expressed by the root excessively or continuously

root	meaning	root + affix	meaning
sigaw	*shout, shouting*	**ka**sisigaw **ka**kasigaw	*excessive or continuous shouting*
isip	*mind, thinking*	**ka**isip **ka**kaisip	*thinking too much*

Sentences:

Napaos si Anne sa kasisigaw.	*Anne was (got) hoarse from all the shouting.*
Hindi' makatulog si Boy sa kaisip kay Nene.	*Boy can't fall asleep because he's thinking of Nene.*

ka-...-an [1]

a person with whom the thing meant by the root is exchanged

root	meaning	root + affix	meaning
sulat	*letter*	kasulatan	*a person with whom letters are exchanged, a correspondent*

| kantyaw | good-natured joke, banter, teasing | kakantyawan | a person with whom jokes are exchanged (someone you tease and who teases you back) |

ka-...-an [2]

an idea or quality expressed in a general, abstract way

root	meaning	root + affix	meaning
bata'	child (boy or girl)	kabataan	youth
ganda	beauty	kagandahan	beauty
bait	kindness	kabaitan	kindness
ligaya	happiness	kaligayahan	happiness
lungkot	sadness	kalungkutan	sadness

Note: As roots expressing a quality may sound ambiguous, the affixed word is preferred in spoken Tagalog. Example:

ang ganda niya	her beauty she's so beautiful*
ang kagandahan niya	her beauty

* See also: Intensifiers and downtoners, Group 2 (p. 259)

ka-...-an [3]

a group of the things meant by the root

root	meaning	root + affix	meaning
bundok	*mountain*	**kabundukan**	*mountain range*
bukid	*field*	**kabukiran**	*fields*
pulo'	*island*	**kapuluan**	*archipelago*

kaka-

See: **ka-** +rep1, **kaka-** (p. 84)

mag-

two persons or things having the relationship expressed by the root

root	meaning	root + affix	meaning
ama	*father*	**mag-ama**	*father and child*
ina	*mother*	**mag-ina**	*mother and child*
bilas	*spouse of one's brother-in-law or sister-in-law (i.e. one's spouse's sibling's spouse)*	**magbilas**	*a person and the spouse of his or her brother-in-law or sister-in-law*
balae	*parent of one's son-in-law or daughter-in-law*	**magbalae**	*a person and a parent of his or her son-in-law or daughter-in-law*

lolo	*grandfather*	**maglolo**	*grandfather and grandchild*
anak	*child*	**mag-anak**	*family (parents and child/children)*
asawa	*spouse*	**mag-asawa**	*husband and wife*
kapatid	*sibling*	**magkapatid**	*two persons who are siblings*
pinsan	*cousin*	**magpinsan**	*two persons who are cousins*

Mag- can also be added to nouns comprising of **ka-** (p. 83) and a root.

root + affix	meaning	root + affixes	meaning
kaklase	*classmate*	**magkaklase**	*two persons who are classmates*
kaopisina	*colleague*	**magkaopisina**	*two persons who are colleagues*

Sentences:

Kumain ang mag-ama.	*The dad and his child ate.*
Mag-ama sila.	*They are father and child.*

mag- +rep1 [1]

three or more persons or things having the relationship expressed by the root

root	meaning	root + affix	meaning
ama	*father*	mag-aama	*father and children*
ina	*mother*	mag-iina	*mother and children*
lola	*grandmother*	maglolola	*grandmother and grandchildren*

Mag- +rep1 [1] can also be added to nouns comprising of **ka-** (p. 83) and a root.

root + affix	meaning	root + affixes	meaning
kaklase	*classmate*	magkakaklase	*three or more persons who are classmates*
kaopisina	*colleague*	magkakaopisina	*three or more persons who are colleagues*

Sentences:

Kumain ang mag-aama.	*The dad and his kids ate.*
Mag-aama sila.	*They are father and children.*

mag- +rep1 [2]

a person associated with the thing or action expressed by the root

root	meaning	root + affix	meaning
nakaw	*something stolen*	magnanakaw	*thief, robber*
taho'	*taho (soy pudding with brown sugar syrup and sago pearls)*	magtataho'	*taho vendor*
balut balot	*balut (boiled duck's egg with a developed embryo)*	magbabalut magbabalot	*balut vendor*
bote	*bottle*	magbobote	*someone who goes from one place to another buying bottles, paper and other recyclables, and then sells them to scrap shops*
saka	*tilling, farming*	magsasaka	*farmer*

mang- +rep1

a person associated with the thing or action expressed by the root

root	meaning	root + affix	meaning
gamot	*medicine*	**manggagamot**	*doctor*
isda'	*fish*	**mangingisda'**	*fisherman*
bayan	*country, town*	**mamamayan**	*citizen*
sayaw	*dance*	**mananayaw**	*dancer*
laro'	*game*	**manlalaro'**	*player*
awit	*song*	**mang-aawit**	*singer*

pa-

the object of an action which has been ordered or requested to be performed

root	meaning	root + affix	meaning
dala	*something brought, bringing*	**padala**	*something ordered or requested to be brought or sent*
gawa'	*work, something made, making, doing*	**pagawa'**	*a task, something ordered or requested to be done*

Sentences:

Padala ni Dora ang regalo.	*The gift was sent by Dora.* Lit. *The gift was something ordered or requested by Dora to be sent.*
Pagawa' ng boss ito.	*The boss wants to have this done.* Lit. *This is something ordered or requested by the boss to be done.*

pa-...-an [1]

a place where the action expressed by the root is performed

root	meaning	root + affix	meaning
aral	*lesson, studying*	**paaralan**	*school*
gawa'	*work, something made*	**pagawaan**	*factory*

pa-...-an [2]

a contest or a competition

root	meaning	root + affix	meaning
ganda	*beauty*	pagandahan	*beauty contest*
taas	*height*	pataasan	*a contest in which the person with the higher or highest score, jump etc. wins*

pag-

the act of doing the action expressed by the root; or,

the manner in which the action expressed by the root is performed

root	meaning	root + affix	meaning
basa	*reading*	pagbasa	*reading*
lakad	*walk, walking*	paglakad	*walking*
luto'	*cuisine, cooking*	pagluto'	*cooking*
sulat	*letter, writing*	pagsulat	*writing*
alis	*departure, leaving*	pag-alis	*leaving*
dating	*arrival, arriving*	pagdating	*arriving*

Note: The root and the affixed word generally mean the same thing.

Mabagal ang _lakad_ niya.	_He/she walks slowly._
Mabagal ang _paglakad_ niya.	Lit. _His/her walking is slow._

pag- +rep1

the act of doing the action expressed by the root repeatedly or habitually

root	meaning	root + affix	meaning
aral	_lesson, studying_	**pag-aaral**	_studying habitually_
basa	_reading_	**pagbabasa**	_reading habitually_
laro'	_game, playing_	**paglalaro'**	_playing habitually_
sulat	_letter, writing_	**pagsusulat**	_writing habitually_

Sentences:

Busy sa pag-aaral si Pong.	_Pong is busy studying._
Dumadalas ang pagsusulat ni Mimi.	_Mimi writes more (and more) frequently._ Lit. _Mimi's writing is becoming more frequent._

pagka-, pagkaka-

the act of having done the action expressed by the root; or,
the manner in which the action expressed by the root was performed

root	meaning	root + affix	meaning
sabi	something said, saying	pagkasabi, pagkakasabi	having said, how something was said
ayos	order, arrangement, arranging	pagkaayos, pagkakaayos	having arranged, how something was arranged

Sentences:

Maliwanag ang pagkakasabi ni Raphael.	*Raphael said it clearly.* Lit. *The way Raphael said it was clear.*
Maganda ang pagkakaayos ng kwarto.	*The room is/was nicely arranged.* Lit. *The way the room was arranged is/was nice.*

pakiki-

a state or quality of being together

root	meaning	root + affix	meaning
sama	*accompanying, coming along*	**pakikisama**	*companionship, getting along well with others, consideration for others*
damay	*helping sympathetically*	**pakikiramay**	*condolence, sympathy*
isa	*one*	**pakikiisa**	*solidarity*

pakikipag-

an action performed with someone

root	meaning	root + affix	meaning
away	*fight*	**pakikipag-away**	*fighting with someone*
usap	*talking*	**pakikipag-usap**	*talking with someone*

Sentences:

Busy sila sa pakikipag-<u>a</u>way.	*They are busy fighting.*
Du<u>ma</u>dalas ang pakikipag-<u>u</u>sap ni Ping kay Bong.	*Ping talks to Bong more (and more) frequently.* Lit. *Ping's talking to Bong is becoming more frequent.*

pang-

a tool or an instrument that is used to perform the action expressed by the root

root	meaning	root + affix	meaning
<u>ba</u>lot	*wrapper, wrapping*	**pam<u>ba</u>lot**	*something that is used to wrap (e.g. gift wrap)*
tanggal	*removed, detached, removing*	**pantanggal**	*remover, something that is used to remove something*
<u>ha</u>lo'	*mixing, stirring*	**pang<u>ha</u>lo'**	*something that is used for mixing or stirring (e.g. a stirring rod, a spoon)*

pang- +rep1

an action or a practice associated with the thing or action expressed by
the root

root	meaning	root + affix	meaning
gamot	*medicine*	panggagamot	*practice of medicine*
anak	*child (son or daughter)*	pananganak	*giving birth, delivery*

tag-

a season

root	meaning	root + affix	meaning
ulan	*rain*	tag-ulan	*rainy season*
init	*heat*	tag-init	*hot season, summer*
araw	*sun*	tag-araw	*summer*
lamig	*cold, coldness*	taglamig	*cold season, winter*

taga- [1]

a native or resident of

root	meaning	root + affix	meaning
New York	*New York*	**taga-New York**	*New Yorker*
probinsya	*province, countryside*	**tagaprobinsya**	*country dweller, someone from the countryside*

taga- [2], tagapag-, tagapang-

a person who performs the action expressed by the root; or,
a person who performs an action associated with the thing expressed by the root

root	meaning	root + affix	meaning
luto'	*cuisine, cooking*	**tagaluto'** **tagapagluto'**	*cook, someone tasked with cooking*
bantay	*guard, guarding*	**tagabantay** **tagapagbantay**	*guard, watcher*
linis	*cleaning*	**tagalinis** **tagapaglinis**	*cleaner, someone tasked with cleaning*
isda'	*fish*	**tagapangisda'**	*someone tasked with fishing*

rep2-...-an

an imitation of the thing meant by the root; a surrogate

root	meaning	root + affix	meaning
<u>ba</u>hay	*house*	bahay-ba<u>ha</u>yan	*playhouse, playing "house" (pretend play)*
<u>ta</u>tay	*father*	tatay-ta<u>ta</u>yan	*stepfather*

Compound nouns

Some nouns are made up of two words, which may or may not be linked by a hyphen.

first word	second word	compound noun
<u>ba</u>hay *house*	bakas<u>yu</u>nan *vacation place*	<u>ba</u>hay-bakas<u>yu</u>nan *vacation home*
anak *child (son or daughter)*	ma<u>ya</u>man *rich*	anak-ma<u>ya</u>man *person born to wealth*

bata' *child (boy or girl)*	lansangan *street*	batang-lansangan* *homeless child*
balik *return*	bayan *town, country*	balikbayan *a Filipino returning to the Philippines either temporarily or for good*

* If the first word ends in a vowel or /n/, **-ng** is added to it. See also: **Na/-ng** (p. 34)

In some cases, the literal meanings of the two component words disappear. Examples:

first word	second word	compound noun
anak *child (son or daughter)*	araw *sun*	anak-araw *albino*
hanap *seeking*	buhay *life*	hanapbuhay *livelihood, work*
bunga *fruit*	araw *sun*	bungang-araw* *prickly heat*
kapit *hold, grasp*	bahay *house*	kapitbahay *neighbor*
kwento *story, tale*	barbero *barber*	kwentong-barbero* *hearsay, tall tale, urban legend* Lit. *barber's tale*

* If the first word ends in a vowel or /n/, **-ng** is added to it. See also: **Na/-ng** (p. 34)

Verbs, adjectives etc. used as nouns

Verbs, adjectives and other parts of speech may also be used as nouns.
Examples:

verb/adjective/etc.		noun	
kumain	*to eat, ate*	**ang kumain**	*the one who ate*
maganda	*pretty*	**ang maganda**	*the pretty one*
nasa school	*in school*	**ang nasa school**	*the one in school*
may kotse	*has a car*	**ang may kotse**	*the one who has a car*
akin	*mine*	**ang akin**	*the one that is mine*

The verb/adjective/etc. may also be preceded by **ng** or **sa**. See also: Ng
markers (p. 45), Sa markers (p. 49)

ng kumain	*(of/by) the one who ate*
sa kumain	*(to etc.) the one who ate*

Examples in plural form:

verb/adjective/etc.		noun	
kumain	to eat, ate	ang mga kumain	the ones who ate
maganda	pretty	ang magaganda, ang mga magaganda	the pretty ones

See also: Plurals (p. 78)

Sentences:

Bago ang nasa school.	*The one in school is new.*
Bago ang akin.	*Mine is new.* Lit. *The one that is mine is new.*
Akin ang bago.	*The new one is mine.*

Verbs used as nouns and their objects

The object of a verb that is used as a noun (p. 101) may be expressed as a Ng phrase (p. 70) or a Sa phrase (p. 70). Examples:

ang kumain ng mangga	*the one who ate a/the mango*
ang kumain sa mangga	*the one who ate the mango*

ang ku**main** nito	*the one who ate this*
ang ku**main** **dito**	*the one who ate this* (can also be understood as *the one who ate here*)

Exception: If the object of a verb that is used as a noun is a personal name* or a personal pronoun, it can only be expressed as a Sa phrase.

ang naka**kita'** kay Grace	*the one who saw Grace*
ang naka**kita'** sa kanya	*the one who saw him/her*

* Personal names are names that refer to specific persons, animals, cartoon characters or anything with a personality.

See also:

- Ang personal pronouns (p. 53)
- Ng personal pronouns (p. 58)
- Sa personal pronouns (p. 63)

Verbs

The basic form

The basic form of a verb is the form one would find in a dictionary. It is made up of a root and one or more affixes.

Example: The verb **kumain** *(to eat)* consists of the root **kain** *(eating)* and the affix **-um-**.

See also: Roots and affixes (p. 29)

Roles of the POD

In sentences with a verb, the role of the POD (p. 35) is indicated by the verb affix. Examples:

Kumain* ng mangga *ang babae.*	*The woman ate a mango.*
	The woman ate some mangoes.

* The affix **-um-** indicates that the POD is the doer of the action.

Ki_na_in* ng ba_ba_e *ang mangga.*	*The woman ate the mango.*
	Lit. *The mango was eaten by the* *woman.*

* The affix **-in-** indicates that the POD is the object of the action.

In sentences with a verb, the POD can take on the role of doer, object, direction, location, beneficiary, instrument, cause or reference of the action.

Note:

1. The direction of an action is the person or thing, for which or in whose direction the action is performed. See also: Difference between direction and object (p. 50)

2. The beneficiary of an action is the person or thing—
   - that benefits from the action, or
   - in whose stead the action is performed.

3. The instrument of an action is the instrument or tool used to perform the action.

4. The reference of an action is what the action is about.

5. In a few cases, the doer of an action is the person or thing experiencing the action, state or condition (the "experiencer" of an action). Examples: **-in** [3] (p. 122), **ma-...-an** [1] (p. 141).

6. In a few cases, the object of an action that is the POD, is the person, animal or thing permitted or asked to perform the action. Examples: **pag-...-in** [1] (p. 195), **papang-...-in** (p. 201).

7. A few verb affixes are used in sentences with no POD. See also: **mag-** [5] (p. 149), **magka-** [1] (p. 155) and **(-)um-** [2] (p. 203).

Sentences:

doer	**Su<u>mu</u>lat sa teacher ang ba<u>bae</u>.**	*The woman wrote (to) the teacher.*
object	**Isi<u>nu</u>lat ng ba<u>bae</u> ang adres.**	*The woman wrote (down) the address.* Lit. *The address was written (down) by the woman.*
direction	**Sinu<u>la</u>tan ng ba<u>bae</u> ang teacher.**	*The woman wrote (to) the teacher.* Lit. *The teacher was written (to) by the woman*
	Sinu<u>la</u>tan ng ba<u>bae</u> ang <u>me</u>sa.	*The woman wrote on the table.* Lit. *The table was written on by the woman.*
location	**Pinagsu<u>la</u>tan ng ba<u>bae</u> ang <u>me</u>sa.**	*The woman wrote at the table.* Lit. *The table was written at by the woman.*
benefi- ciary	**Ipinagsulat ng ba<u>bae</u> ang <u>ba</u>ta'.**	*The woman wrote for (on behalf of) the child.* Lit. *The child was written for by the woman.*
instru- ment	**Ipinang<u>su</u>lat ng ba<u>bae</u> ang ballpen.**	*The woman used the pen to write.* Lit. *The pen was written with by the woman.*

cause	**Ikinagalit ng babae ang sitwasyon.**	*The woman got angry because of the situation.* Lit. *The situation caused the woman to get angry.*
reference	**Pinag-usapan nila *ang sitwasyon.***	*They talked about the situation.* Lit. *The situation was talked about by them.*

Verb affixes

The most common verb affixes are given below, together with a number of examples of verbs, verb forms and sentences.

The different verb forms indicate aspect. That is, they indicate whether the action has been started or not, and, if started, whether it has been completed or not. For an overview of the aspects and the rules for indicating them, see Aspects (p. 206).

Not all roots can be combined with any given affix.

The roots and root-affix combinations may have more meanings than the ones given here.

See also:

- Roots and affixes (p. 29)
- Sound changes when combining roots and affixes (p. 31)
- Syllable repetition (p. 33)

-an [1]

POD: object

to do something to a person or a thing (expresses various kinds of actions)

root	meaning	root + affix	meaning
bukas	open	buksan	to open
balat	skin	balatan	to peel
hugas	washing	hugasan	to wash
walis	broom	walisan	to sweep
tanda'	remembering, marker	tandaan	to remember
haya'	tolerating	hayaan	to let be

Aspects:

basic form	completed	uncompleted	unstarted
buksan	binuksan	binubuksan	bubuksan
hugasan	hinugasan	hinuhugasan	huhugasan

Sentences:

Binuksan ni Mary ang pinto'.	Mary opened the door.
Hinugasan ni Alfred ang pinggan.	Alfred did (washed) the dishes.

-an [2]

POD: object

to cause something to become; *to make*

root	meaning	root + affix	meaning
ganda	*beauty*	gandahan	*to make beautiful or nice*
tamis	*sweetness*	tamisan	*to make sweet, to sweeten*
bagal	*slowness*	bagalan	*to make slow, to slow down*

Aspects:

basic form	completed	uncompleted	unstarted
tamisan	ti*n*amisan	ti*na*tamisan	*ta*tamisan
bagalan	bi*n*agalan	bi*na*bagalan	*ba*bagalan

Sentences:

Tinamisan ni Ralph ang juice.	*Ralph sweetened the juice.*
Binagalan ni Elvira ang kotse.	*Elvira slowed down the car.*

-an [3]

POD: direction

to do something in the (physical or psychological) direction of

root	meaning	root + affix	meaning
lapit	*closeness*	lapitan	*to approach*
punta	*direction, destination*	puntahan	*to go to*
pasyal	*stroll, walk, visit*	pasyalan	*to visit*
upo'	*sitting*	upuan	*to sit down on*
abot	*reach, within reach*	abutan	*to pass to*
dala	*bringing, something brought*	dalhan	*to take/bring to*
sulat	*letter, writing*	sulatan	*to write to*
tawag	*call*	tawagan	*to call (to phone)*
lagay	*something put*	lagyan	*to put in/on*
bigay	*something given*	bigyan	*to give*
tingin	*look*	tingnan	*to look at*
ihip	*blowing*	hipan (irregular verb)	*to blow on*
ngiti'	*smile*	ngitian	*to smile at*

tawa	laughter	ta<u>wa</u>nan	to laugh at
kanta	song	kantahan	to sing to
halik	kiss	halikan	to kiss
<u>tu</u>long	help	tu<u>lu</u>ngan	to help
sakit	pain	saktan	to hurt

Aspects:

basic form	completed	uncompleted	unstarted
puntahan	pi*n*untahan	pi<u>*nu*</u>puntahan	<u>*pu*</u>puntahan
tingnan	ti*n*ingnan	ti<u>*ni*</u>tingnan	<u>*ti*</u>tingnan

Sentences:

Pinuntahan ni John si Paul.	*John went to Paul.*
Tiningnan ni Tom ang picture.	*Tom looked at the picture.*

-an [4]

POD: beneficiary
to do something for

root	meaning	root + affix	meaning
tira	*leftover*	tirhan	*to leave something for*
<u>i</u>wan	*leaving*	i<u>wa</u>nan	*to leave something for*

Aspects:

basic form	completed	uncompleted	unstarted
tirhan	ti*n*irhan	ti*ni*tirhan	*ti*tirhan
i*wa*nan	i*ni wa*nan	i*ni*i*wa*nan	*ii*wanan

Sentences:

Tinirhan ni Ben ng cake si Anne.	*Ben left some cake for Anne.*
Iniwanan ni Ben ng ice cream si Anne.	*Ben left some ice cream for Anne.*

-an +rep2 [1]

POD: object
to do something occasionally, at random, a little, a bit, now and then or here and there

root	meaning	root + affix	meaning
walis	*broom*	**walis-walisan**	*to sweep a little (etc.)*
tamis	*sweetness*	**tamis-tamisan**	*to sweeten a bit (etc.)*
bagal	*slowness*	**bagal-bagalan**	*to slow down a bit (etc.)*

Aspects:

basic form	completed	uncompleted	unstarted
tamis-tamisan	ti*n*amis-tamisan	ti*na*tamis-tamisan	*ta*tamis-tamisan
bagal-ba*ga*lan	bi*n*agal-ba*ga*lan	bi*na*bagal-ba*ga*lan	*ba*bagal-ba*ga*lan

Sentences:

Tinamis-tamisan ni Ralph ang juice.	*Ralph sweetened the juice a bit.*
Binagal-ba<u>ga</u>lan ni Elvira ang <u>ko</u>tse.	*Elvira slowed the car down a little.*

-an +rep2 [2]

POD: direction
to do something in the (physical or psychological) direction of, occasionally, at random, a little, a bit, now and then or here and there

root	meaning	root + affix	meaning
<u>tu</u>long	*help*	tulung-tu<u>lu</u>ngan	*to help a little (etc.)*
tingin	*look*	tingnan-tingnan	*to look at now and then (etc.)*

Aspects:

basic form	completed	uncompleted	unstarted
tulung-tul*un*gan	ti*n*ulung-tul*un*gan	ti*nu*tulung-tul*un*gan	*tu*tulung-tul*un*gan
tingnan-tingnan	ti*n*ingnan-tingnan	ti*ni*tingnan-tingnan	*ti*tingnan-tingnan

Sentences:

Tinulung-tul*un*gan ni Dora si Rick.	*Dora helped Rick a bit.*
Tiningnan-tingnan ni Carina ang nil*ag*a'.	*Carina looked at the stew occasionally.*

i- 1

POD: object
to do something to a person or a thing (expresses various kinds of actions)

root	meaning	root + affix	meaning
t*a*pon	*throwing*	**it*a*pon**	*to throw (away)*
bigay	*something given*	**ibigay**	*to give*
akyat	*going up*	**iakyat**	*to bring/take up*
uwi'	*going/coming home*	**iuwi'**	*to take home*
t*a*go'	*hiding*	**it*a*go'**	*to hide (something)*

tanim	*something planted*	itanim	*to plant*
s<u>u</u>lat	*letter, writing*	is<u>u</u>lat	*to write (down)*
sara	*closing*	isara	*to close*
s<u>a</u>ma	*joining, including*	is<u>a</u>ma	*to include*
dagdag	*adding*	idagdag	*to add*
balik	*returning*	ibalik	*to return (something)*
lagay	*something put*	ilagay	*to put*

Aspects:

basic form	completed	uncompleted	unstarted
isara	(i)si*n*ara	(i)si*na*sara	is*a*sara
i<u>t</u>apon	(i)ti*n*apon	(i)ti*na*tapon	it*a*tapon

Sentences:

Sinara ni Chris ang pinto'.	*Chris closed the door.*
Ti<u>na</u>pon ni Rose ang envelope.	*Rose threw the envelope away.*

i- [2]

POD: beneficiary

to do something for

root	meaning	root + affix	meaning
bili	*buying, buying price*	ibili	*to buy something for*
kumusta	*how (is/are)*	ikumusta	*to say hello for*
k<u>u</u>ha'	*getting*	ik<u>u</u>ha'	*to get something for*
<u>ha</u>nap	*something sought*	i<u>ha</u>nap	*to search for (the benefit of)*

Aspects:

basic form	completed	uncompleted	unstarted
ibili	(i)bi*n*ili	(i)bi<u>ni</u>bili	i<u>bi</u>bili
ikumusta	(i)ki*n*umusta	(i)ki<u>nu</u>kumusta	ik<u>u</u>kumusta

Sentences:

Ibinili ni Alfred ng cake si Natalie.	*Alfred bought Natalie some cake.*
Ki<u>nu</u>kumusta ni Tony si Elena.	*Tony says hello (sends his greetings) to Elena.*

i- +rep2

POD: object

to do something occasionally, at random, a little, a bit, now and then or here and there

root	meaning	root + affix	meaning
urong	*moving back*	iurong-urong	*to move (something) back a little (etc.)*
handa'	*ready, prepared*	ihanda-handa'	*to prepare (something) a little (etc.)*

Aspects:

basic form	completed	uncompleted	unstarted
iurong-urong	*in*urong-urong *in*iurong-urong	*inu*urong-urong *ini*uurong-urong	i*u*urong-urong
ihanda-handa'	(i)h*in*anda-handa'	(i)h*ina*handa-handa'	ih*a*handa-handa'

Sentences:

Inurong-urong ni Rene ang kotse.	*Rene moved back the car a little.*
Hinanda-handa' ni Marge ang kwarto.	*Marge prepared the room a bit.*

ika-

POD: cause

to cause, to be the cause of

root	meaning	root + affix	meaning
ga_lit	*anger*	ikaga_lit	*to cause someone to get angry*
patay	*dead*	ikamatay	*to cause someone's death*

Aspects:

basic form	completed	uncompleted	unstarted
ikaga_lit	(i)kinaga_lit	(i)ki_na_kaga_lit	ika_kaga_lit
ikamatay	(i)ki_namatay	(i)ki_na_kamatay	ika_kamatay

Sentences:

Kinaga_lit ni Mike ang ba_lita'.	*Mike got angry because of the news.*
Kinamatay ng teacher ang aksi_dente.	*The teacher died because of the accident.*

-in [1]

POD: object

to do something to a person or a thing (expresses various kinds of actions)

root	meaning	root + affix	meaning
kain	*eating*	kainin	*to eat*
inom	*drinking*	inumin	*to drink*
mahal	*someone loved*	mahalin	*to love*
basa	*reading*	basahin	*to read*
luto'	*cooking, cuisine*	lutuin	*to cook*
tapos	*finished*	tapusin	*to finish*
sabi	*something said*	sabihin	*to say, to tell*
linis	*cleaning*	linisin	*to clean*
tawag	*call*	tawagin	*to call*
alis	*removing*	alisin	*to remove*
isip	*mind*	isipin	*to think about*
gising	*waking up*	gisingin	*to wake (someone) up*

Aspects:

basic form	completed	uncompleted	unstarted
kainin	kinain	kinakain	kakainin
sabihin	sinabi	sinasabi	sasabihin

120　*Essential Tagalog Grammar*

Sentences:

Ki<u>na</u>in ni Mark ang mangga.	*Mark ate the mango.*
Si<u>na</u>bi ni John ang totoo.	*John told the truth.*

-in ²

POD: direction
to do something in the (physical or psychological) direction of

root	meaning	root + affix	meaning
<u>pa</u>sok	*entering*	**pa<u>su</u>kin**	*to enter*
<u>da</u>law	*visit*	**da<u>la</u>win**	*to visit*
suntok	*punch*	**suntukin**	*to punch*

Aspects:

basic form	completed	uncompleted	unstarted
pa<u>su</u>kin	*pi<u>na</u>sok*	*pi<u>na</u>pasok*	*<u>pa</u>pa<u>su</u>kin*
da<u>la</u>win	*di<u>na</u>law*	*di<u>na</u>dalaw*	*<u>da</u>da<u>la</u>win*

Sentences:

Pi<u>na</u>sok ng magna<u>na</u>kaw ang <u>ba</u>hay.	*The burglar entered the house.*
Di<u>na</u>law ni Peter si Heidi.	*Peter visited Heidi.*

-in [3]

POD: doer

to be affected or overtaken by a condition, feeling or phenomenon

Note: In this and a few other cases, the "doer of an action" is the person or thing experiencing the action, state or condition.

root	meaning	root + affix	meaning
baha'	*flood*	bahain	*to be flooded*
bagyo	*typhoon, storm*	bagyuhin	*to be overtaken by a storm*
gabi	*night*	gabihin	*to be overtaken by darkness or night, to be late (used in the evening/night)*
tanghali'	*noon*	tanghaliin	*to be overtaken by noon, to be late (used in the morning)*
antok	*sleepiness*	antukin	*to get sleepy*
gutom	*hunger*	gutumin	*to starve*
uhaw	*thirst*	uhawin	*to get thirsty*
ginaw	*cold*	ginawin	*to feel cold*
sipon	*a cold*	sipunin	*to catch or have a cold*

a<u>ta</u>ke	*attack*	ata<u>ki</u>hin	*to have an attack of, to suffer an attack*
kapos	*insufficient*	kapusin	*to be (caught) short*

Aspects:

basic form	completed	uncompleted	unstarted
sipunin	si*n*ipon	si*ni*sipon	*si*sipunin
bahain	bi*n*aha'	bi*na*baha'	*ba*bahain
gabihin	gi*n*abi	gi*na*gabi	*ga*gabihin

Sentences:

Sinipon si John.	*John caught a cold.*
Binaha' ang <u>ba</u>hay.	*The house was flooded.*
Ginabi si Grace.	*It was already dark/late in the evening/late at night when Grace did something.* Lit. *Grace was overtaken by night (was late).*
Ginabi ng dating si Grace.	*It was already dark/late in the evening/late at night when Grace arrived.* Lit. *Grace was overtaken by night (was late) in arriving.*
Kinapos ng <u>pe</u>ra si John.	*John ran short of money.*

-in +rep2

POD: object
to do something occasionally, at random, a little, a bit, now and then or
here and there

root	meaning	root + affix	meaning
linis	*cleaning*	linis-linisin	*to clean a little (etc.)*
isip	*mind*	isip-isipin	*to think about or consider a little (etc.)*

Aspects:

basic form	completed	uncompleted	unstarted
linis-linisin	*ni*linis-linis	*nili*linis-linis	*li*linis-linisin
isip-isipin	*ini*sip-isip	*inii*sip-isip	*i*isip-isipin

Sentences:

Nilinis-linis ni Katrina ang garahe.	*Katrina cleaned the garage a bit.*
Inisip-isip ni Walter iyon.	*Walter thought a bit about that.*

ipa-

POD: object
to let, make or have someone do something

root	meaning	root + affix	meaning
hiram	*borrowing*	ipahiram	*to let someone borrow something, to lend*
luto'	*cooking, cuisine*	ipaluto'	*to make someone cook something*
kain	*eating*	ipakain	*to make someone or an animal eat something*
linis	*cleaning*	ipalinis	*to make someone clean something*
kita'	*seeing*	ipakita'	*to make or let someone see something, to show*

Aspects:

basic form	completed	uncompleted	unstarted
ipahiram	(i)pi*n*ahiram	(i)*pina*pahiram	i*pa*pahiram
ipakita'	(i)pi*n*akita'	(i)*pina*pakita'	i*pa*pakita'

Sentences:

Pinahiram ni Peter kay Heidi ang libro.	*Peter lent the book to Heidi.*
Pina<u>ki</u>ta' ni Andrew kay Mike ang picture.	*Andrew showed Mike the picture.*

ipag- [1]

POD: beneficiary

to do something for

root	meaning	root + affix	meaning
<u>lu</u>to'	*cooking, cuisine*	**ipag<u>lu</u>to'**	*to cook for*
<u>la</u>ban	*against, fighting*	**ipag<u>la</u>ban**	*to fight for, to stand up for*
laba	*washing of clothes*	**ipaglaba**	*to wash clothes for*

Aspects:

basic form	completed	uncompleted	unstarted
ipag<u>lu</u>to'	(i)pi*n*ag<u>lu</u>to'	(i)*pina*pag<u>lu</u>to'	i*pa*pag<u>lu</u>to'
ipag<u>la</u>ban	(i)pi*n*ag<u>la</u>ban	(i)*pina*pag<u>la</u>ban	i*pa*pag<u>la</u>ban

Sentences:

| Pinag<u>lu</u>to' ni David si Gina. | *David cooked for Gina.* |
| Pinag<u>la</u>ban ni Jay si Sarah. | *Jay stood up for Sarah.* |

ipag- 2
POD: object
to do something to a thing

root	meaning	root + affix	meaning
bili	*buying price*	ipagbili	*to sell*
palit	*changing*	ipagpalit	*to replace with*
tapat	*faithful*	ipagtapat	*to confess*

Aspects:

basic form	completed	uncompleted	unstarted
ipagbili	(i)pi*n*agbili	(i)pi*na*pagbili (i)pi*n*ag*bi*bili	i*pa*pagbili ipag*bi*bili
ipagtapat	(i)pi*n*agtapat	(i)pi*na*pagtapat (i)pi*n*ag*ta*tapat	i*pa*pagtapat ipag*ta*tapat

Sentences:

| Pinagbili ni Sandra ang bag. | *Sandra sold the bag.* |
| Pinag<u>t</u>apat ni John ang lahat. | *John confessed everything.* |

ipag- +rep1

POD: object

to do something repeatedly, continually, a lot, intensively or frequently; or, to do something involving multiple objects

root	meaning	root + affix	meaning
<u>ta</u>pon	*throwing away*	ipagtatapon	*to throw repeatedly (etc.)*
balik	*returning*	ipagbabalik	*to return (many things) (etc.)*

Aspects:

basic form	completed	uncompleted	unstarted
ipagtatapon	(i)pi*n*agta-tapon	(i)pi*n*ag<u>ta</u>tatapon (i)*pina*pagtatapon	ipag<u>ta</u>tatapon i*pa*pagtatapon
ipagbabalik	(i)pi*n*agba-balik	(i)pi*n*ag<u>ba</u>babalik (i)*pina*pagbabalik	ipag<u>ba</u>babalik i*pa*pagbabalik

Sentences:

Pinagtatapon ni Jay ang mga box.	*Jay threw away the boxes (and there were many of them).*
Pinagbabalik ni Maria kay John ang mga re<u>ga</u>lo.	*Maria gave the gifts back to John (and there were many of them).*

ipang- [1]

POD: instrument
to do something using

root	meaning	root + affix	meaning
luto'	cooking, cuisine	ipanluto'	to use something to cook
halo'	mixing	ipanghalo'	to use something to stir/mix
hiwa'	slicing	ipanghiwa'	to use something to slice
punas	wiping	ipampunas	to use something to wipe

Aspects:

basic form	completed	uncompleted	unstarted
ipanluto'	(i)pinanluto'	(i)pinapanluto' (i)pinanluluto'	ipapanluto' ipanluluto'
ipanghalo'	(i)pinanghalo'	(i)pinapanghalo' (i)pinanghahalo'	ipapanghalo' ipanghahalo'

Sentences:

| Pinan<u>lut</u>o' ni Hilda ang kut<u>sa</u>ra. | *Hilda cooked with the spoon.* |
| Pinang<u>ha</u>lo' ni John sa iced tea ang straw. | *John stirred the iced tea with the straw.* |

ipang- [2]

POD: object

to do something to a person or a thing

root	meaning	root + affix	meaning
anak	*child (son or daughter)*	ipanganak	*to give birth to*
<u>a</u>ko'	*promise* (rarely used)	ipa<u>nga</u>ko'	*to promise*

Aspects:

basic form	completed	uncompleted	unstarted
ipanganak	(i)pi*n*anganak	(i)*pi<u>na</u>*panganak (i)pina<u>nga</u>nganak	ipapanganak ipa<u>nga</u>nganak
ipa<u>nga</u>ko'	(i)pi*n*a<u>nga</u>ko'	(i)*pi<u>na</u>*pangako' (i)pina<u>nga</u>ngako'	ipapangako' ipa<u>nga</u>ngako'

Sentences:

Pinanganak ni Teodora si Rizal noong 1861.	*Teodora gave birth to Rizal in 1861.*
Pinangako' ni John iyon.	*John promised that.*

ka-...-an [1]

POD: location
to do something in/on/at; or,
to occur in/on/at

root	meaning	root + affix	meaning
patay	*dead*	**kamatayan**	*to die in*
lunod	*drowning*	**kalunuran**	*to drown in*

Aspects:

basic form	completed	uncompleted	unstarted
kamatayan	**ki***n***amatayan**	***kina*kamatayan** **ki***nama*matayan**	***ka*kamatayan** **ka***ma*matayan**
kalu*nu*ran**	**ki***n***alu***nu*ran**	***kina*kalu***nu*ran** **ki***na*lu*lu***nu*ran**	***ka*kalu***nu*ran** **ka***lu*lu***nu*ran**

Sentences:

Kinamatayan ni Magellan ang dalampasigan.	*Magellan died on the shore.*
Kinalunuran ng babae ang ilog.	*The woman drowned in the river.*

ka-...-an ²

POD: direction
to feel or experience something

root	meaning	root + affix	meaning
limot	*oblivion*	**kalimutan**	*to forget (to stop thinking about or remembering), to neglect*
galit	*anger*	**kagalitan**	*to be angry with, to scold*

Aspects:

basic form	completed	uncompleted	unstarted
kalimutan	ki*na*limutan	*kina*kali*mu*tan kina*li*li*mu*tan	*ka*kali*mu*tan ka*li*li*mu*tan
kagalitan	ki*na*galitan	*kina*kaga*li*tan kina*ga*ga*li*tan	*ka*kaga*li*tan kag*a*ga*li*tan

Sentences:

Kinali<u>mu</u>tan ni Maria ang ex niya.	*Maria forgot about her ex.*
Kinaga<u>li</u>tan ni Susan si Juan.	*Susan scolded Juan.*

ma- [1]

POD: doer

to do something (expresses various kinds of actions)

root	meaning	root + affix	meaning
<u>tu</u>log	*sleep*	**ma<u>tu</u>log**	*to sleep*
<u>li</u>go'	*bathing*	**ma<u>li</u>go'**	*to take a shower or a bath, to wash (one's body)*
kinig	*something heard*	**makinig**	*to listen*
higa'	*lying down*	**mahiga'**	*to lie down*
upo'	*sitting*	**maupo'**	*to sit down*

Aspects:

basic form	completed	uncompleted	unstarted
ma<u>tu</u>log	*n*a<u>tu</u>log	*n*a<u>tu</u>tulog	ma<u>tu</u>tulog
makinig	*n*akinig	*n*a<u>ki</u>kinig	ma<u>ki</u>kinig

Sentences:

Na**tu**log si Hilda.	*Hilda slept.*
Nakinig si Jeanne sa **ra**dyo.	*Jeanne listened to the radio.*

ma- [2]

POD: doer
to do something unintentionally; or,
to get into a certain state unintentionally

root	meaning	root + affix	meaning
dulas	*slipperiness*	madulas	*to slip*
bangga'	*colliding*	mabangga'	*to bump or collide (with)*
hulog	*falling*	ma**hu**log	*to fall*
gutom	*hunger*	ma**gu**tom	*to get hungry*
patay	*dead*	mamatay	*to die*
bingi	*deaf*	mabingi	*to become deaf*
huli	*late*	mahuli	*to be late*
basag	*a crack*	ma**ba**sag	*to crack or break*
sira'	*damage*	ma**si**ra'	*to get damaged*

Aspects:

basic form	completed	uncompleted	unstarted
madulas	*n*adulas	*n*a*du*dulas	ma*du*dulas
mahuli	*n*ahuli	*n*a*hu*huli	ma*hu*huli

Sentences:

Nadulas si John.	*John slipped.*
Nahuli si Mike.	*Mike was late.*

ma- 3

POD: doer
to feel an emotion

root	meaning	root + affix	meaning
tuwa'	*joy, happiness*	matuwa'	*to become happy*
lungkot	*sadness*	malungkot	*to become sad*
takot	*fear*	matakot	*to be afraid*
galit	*anger*	magalit	*to get angry*
hiya'	*shame*	mahiya'	*to be embarrassed, to be ashamed, to be shy*

gulat	surprise	magulat	to be surprised, to be startled
inis	annoyance	mainis	to be annoyed

Aspects:

basic form	completed	uncompleted	unstarted
mahiya'	nahiya'	nahihiya'	mahihiya'
magulat	nagulat	nagugulat	magugulat

Sentences:

Nahiya' si Natalie.	Natalie felt shy.
Nagulat si Alfred.	Alfred was startled.

ma- [4]

POD: object
to be able to do something to a person or a thing

root	meaning	root + affix	meaning
kain	eating	makain	to be able to eat
kita'	seeing	makita'	to (be able to) see
sabi	something said	masabi	to be able to say

alaala	memory	maalala (irregular verb)	to (be able to) remember
rinig	hearing	marinig	to (be able to) hear
bili	buying price, buying	mabili	to be able to buy
basa	reading	mabasa	to be able to read
kuha'	getting	makuha'	to be able to get

Aspects:

basic form	completed	uncompleted	unstarted
maalala	naalala	naaalala	maaalala
mabasa	nabasa	nababasa	mababasa

Sentences:

Naalala ni Grace ang password.	Grace remembered the password.
Nabasa ni Ralph ang sign.	Ralph was able to read the sign.

ma- [5]

POD: object

to do something involuntarily or accidentally

root	meaning	root + affix	meaning
ka̱in	*eating*	ma**ka̱in**	*to eat unintentionally*
sa̱bi	*something said*	ma**sa̱bi**	*to say unintentionally*
su̱nog	*fire*	ma**su̱nog**	*to burn unintentionally*
ba̱sag	*a crack*	ma**ba̱sag**	*to crack or break*
ala**a̱la**	*memory*	maa**la̱la** (irregular verb)	*to remember unintentionally*
rinig	*hearing*	ma**rinig**	*to hear unintentionally*

Aspects:

basic form	completed	uncompleted	unstarted
ma**ka̱in**	*n*a**ka̱in**	*n*a**ka̱**ka̱in	ma**ka̱**ka̱in
ma**ba̱sag**	*n*a**ba̱sag**	*n*a**ba̱**ba̱sag	ma**ba̱**ba̱sag

Sentences:

| Na<u>kai</u>n ni Jose ang buto. | *Jose accidentally swallowed (ate) the pit.* |
| Na<u>ba</u>sag ni Yoyoy ang <u>ba</u>so. | *Yoyoy accidentally broke the (drinking) glass.* |

ma- [6]

POD: object
to perceive something

root	meaning	root + affix	meaning
<u>ki</u>ta'	*seeing*	ma<u>ki</u>ta'	*to see*
halata'	*noticeable, obvious*	mahalata'	*to detect, to notice*

Aspects:

basic form	completed	uncompleted	unstarted
ma<u>ki</u>ta'	*n*a<u>ki</u>ta'	*n*a<u>kiki</u>ta'	ma<u>kiki</u>ta'
mahalata'	*n*ahalata'	*n*a<u>ha</u>halata'	ma<u>ha</u>halata'

Sentences:

| Na<u>ki</u>ta' ni Ralph si Elvira. | *Ralph saw Elvira.* |
| Nahalata' ni Mary iyon. | *Mary noticed that.* |

ma- +rep2

POD: doer

to do or feel something slightly, a little or a bit

root	meaning	root + affix	meaning
hiya'	*shame*	mahiya-hiya'	*to be a bit ashamed, to be a bit shy (etc.)*
higa'	*lying down*	mahiga-higa'	*to lie down a little (etc.)*

Aspects:

basic form	completed	uncompleted	unstarted
mahiya-hiya'	*n*ahiya-hiya'	*n*ahihiya-hiya'	ma*hi*hiya-hiya'
mahiga-higa'	*n*ahiga-higa'	*n*ahihiga-higa'	ma*hi*higa-higa'

Sentences:

Nahihiya-hiya' si Edmond.	*Edmond is feeling a bit shy.*
Nahiga-higa' si Theresa.	*Theresa lay down for a little while.*

ma-...-an [1]

POD: doer

to experience a quality or a condition

Note: In this and a few other cases, the "doer of an action" is the person or thing experiencing the action, state or condition.

root	meaning	root + affix	meaning
sira'	*damage*	masiraan	*to have something break down on someone*
wala'	*nothing*	mawalan	*to have something disappear on someone, to lose something*
ubos	*used up*	maubusan	*to have something run out on someone, to run out of*

Aspects:

basic form	completed	uncompleted	unstarted
masiraan	*n*asiraan	*n*as*i*siraan	mas*i*siraan
mawalan	*n*awalan	*n*a*wa*walan	ma*wa*walan

Sentences:

Nasiraan si John.	*Something broke down on John.* Lit. *John had something break down on him.*
Nasiraan ng kotse si John.	*John's car broke down on him.* Lit. *John had a car break down on him.*
Nawalan si John.	*John lost something.* Lit. *John had something disappear on him.*
Nawalan ng pag-asa si John.	*John lost hope.* Lit. *John had hope disappear on him.*
Naubusan si John.	*John ran out of something.* Lit. *John had something run out on him.*
Naubusan ng pera si John.	*John ran out of money.* Lit. *John had money run out on him.*

ma-...-an [2]

POD: doer

to feel a particular way about something

root	meaning	root + affix	meaning
anghang	*spiciness (pungency)*	**maanghangan**	*to find something spicy (hot)*
_a_lat	*saltiness*	**maa_la_tan**	*to find something salty*
lamig	*cold*	**malamigan**	*to find something cold, to feel the cold*
_i_nit	*heat*	**mai_ni_tan**	*to find something hot, to feel hot*
gulo	*chaos, confusion*	**maguluhan**	*to find something chaotic or confusing*

Aspects:

basic form	completed	uncompleted	unstarted
maanghangan	**_n_aanghangan**	**na_a_anghangan**	**ma_a_anghangan**
maguluhan	**_n_aguluhan**	**na_gu_guluhan**	**ma_gu_guluhan**

Sentences:

Naanghangan si Lorraine sa sauce.	*Lorraine found the sauce (too) spicy.*
Naguluhan si Joey sa tanong.	*Joey found the question confusing.*

ma-...-an [3]

POD: object
to feel or experience something

root	meaning	root + affix	meaning
tuto	*learning*	matutunan	*to learn*
damdam	*feeling*	maramdaman	*to feel*

Aspects:

basic form	completed	uncompleted	unstarted
matutunan	natutunan	natututunan	matututunan
maramdaman	naramdaman	nararamdaman	mararamdaman

Sentences:

Natutunan ni Bryan ang pagmamaneho.	*Bryan learned how to drive (driving).*
Naramdaman ni Ed ang lindol.	*Ed felt the earthquake.*

mag- [1]

POD: doer

to do something (expresses various kinds of actions)

root	meaning	root + affix	meaning
luto'	*cooking, cuisine*	**magluto'**	*to cook*
aral	*lesson, studying*	**mag-aral**	*to study*
lakad	*walking*	**maglakad**	*to walk*
sulat	*writing, letter*	**magsulat**	*to write*
bigay	*giving*	**magbigay**	*to give*
laro'	*game*	**maglaro'**	*to play*
isip	*mind*	**mag-isip**	*to think*
linis	*cleaning*	**maglinis**	*to clean*
tanong	*question*	**magtanong**	*to ask*

Aspects:

basic form	completed	uncompleted	unstarted
magluto'	*n*agluto'	*n*ag*lu*luto'	mag*lu*luto'
maglakad	*n*aglakad	*n*ag*la*lakad	mag*la*lakad

Sentences:

| Nag<u>lu</u>to' si Mary. | *Mary cooked.* |
| Naglakad si Alfred. | *Alfred walked.* |

mag- [2]

POD: doer

to take up an occupation

root	meaning	root + affix	meaning
doktor	*doctor*	magdoktor	*to become a doctor*
ar<u>tis</u>ta	*actor, actress*	mag-ar<u>tis</u>ta	*to become an actor or an actress*

Aspects:

basic form	completed	uncompleted	unstarted
magdoktor	*n*agdoktor	*n*ag<u>*do*</u>doktor	mag<u>*do*</u>doktor
mag-ar<u>tis</u>ta	*n*ag-ar<u>tis</u>ta	*n*ag-<u>*a*</u>ar<u>tis</u>ta	mag-<u>*a*</u>ar<u>tis</u>ta

Sentences:

| Mag<u>do</u>doktor si Arthur. | *Arthur will become a doctor.* |
| Nag-ar<u>tis</u>ta si John. | *John became an actor.* |

mag- [3]

POD: doer

to use or wear something

root	meaning	root + affix	meaning
bus	*bus*	**magbus**	*to take a bus*
shorts	*shorts*	**magshorts**	*to wear shorts*
Tagalog	*Tagalog*	**mag-Tagalog**	*to speak Tagalog*
French	*French*	**mag-French**	*to speak French*
sigarilyo	*cigarette*	**magsigarilyo**	*to smoke*

Aspects:

basic form	completed	uncompleted	unstarted
magbus	**_n_agbus**	**_n_ag_u_bus**	**mag_u_bus**
mag-Tagalog	**_n_ag-Tagalog**	**_n_ag_ta_-Tagalog**	**mag_ta_-Tagalog**

Sentences:

Nagbus si Madeline.	*Madeline took a bus.*
Nag_ta_-Tagalog si Michelle.	*Michelle speaks Tagalog.*

mag- [4]

POD: doer

to perform a reciprocal action

root	meaning	root + affix	meaning
<u>u</u>sap	*talking*	mag-<u>u</u>sap	*to talk to each other*
<u>a</u>way	*quarreling*	mag-<u>a</u>way	*to quarrel with each other*
hiwalay	*separated*	maghiwalay	*to separate from each other*
<u>ki</u>ta'	*seeing*	mag<u>ki</u>ta'	*to see each other*

Aspects:

basic form	completed	uncompleted	unstarted
mag-<u>u</u>sap	*n*ag-<u>u</u>sap	*n*ag-*uu*sap	mag-*uu*sap
mag<u>ki</u>ta'	*n*ag<u>ki</u>ta'	*n*ag*ki*<u>ki</u>ta'	mag*ki*<u>ki</u>ta'

Sentences:

Nag-<u>u</u>sap sina Val at Carina.	*Val and Carina talked to each other.*
Nag<u>ki</u>ta' sina Tom at Chris.	*Tom and Chris saw each other.*

mag- [5]

POD: none
to be

root	meaning	root + affix	meaning
December	December	mag-December	to be December
Pasko	Christmas	mag-Pasko	to be Christmas
three o'clock	three o'clock	mag-three o'clock	to be three o'clock
twenty-five	twenty-five	mag-twenty-five	to be the 25th

Aspects:

basic form	completed	uncompleted	unstarted
mag-Pasko	nag-Pasko	nagpa-Pasko	magpa-Pasko
mag-December	nag-December	nagde-December	magde-December

Sentences:

Magpa-Pasko na!	It will soon be Christmas!
Magde-December na.	It will soon be December.

mag- +rep1

POD: doer

to do something repeatedly, continually, a lot, intensively or frequently

root	meaning	root + affix	meaning
iyak	*crying*	mag-iiyak	*to cry repeatedly (etc.)*
paniwala'	*belief*	magpapaniwala'	*to believe repeatedly (etc.)*
sigaw	*shouting*	magsisigaw	*to shout repeatedly, to scream repeatedly (etc.)*
daldal	*chatter*	magdadaldal	*to chatter repeatedly (etc.)*

Aspects:

basic form	completed	uncompleted	unstarted
magsisigaw	*n*agsisigaw	*n*ag*si*sisigaw	mag*si*sisigaw
magpapaniwala'	*n*agpapaniwala'	*n*ag*pa*pa-paniwala'	mag*pa*pa-paniwala'

Sentences:

Nagsisigaw ang ba<u>ba</u>e.	*The woman was shouting and screaming.*
Nag<u>pa</u>papapaniwala′ sila sa <u>tsis</u>mis.	*They keep believing rumors (or gossip).*

mag- +rep2 [1]

POD: doer

to perform a reciprocal action involving three or more doers

root	meaning	root + affix	meaning
<u>ki</u>ta′	*seeing*	mag<u>ki</u>ta-<u>ki</u>ta′	*to see one another*
hiwalay	*separated*	maghi<u>wa</u>-hiwalay	*to separate from one another*
<u>u</u>sap	*talking*	mag-<u>u</u>sap-<u>u</u>sap	*to talk to one another*

Aspects:

basic form	completed	uncompleted	unstarted
mag<u>ki</u>ta-<u>ki</u>ta′	*n*ag<u>ki</u>ta-<u>ki</u>ta′	*n*ag*ki*<u>ki</u>ta-<u>ki</u>ta′	mag*ki*<u>ki</u>ta-<u>ki</u>ta′
maghi<u>wa</u>-hiwalay	*n*aghi<u>wa</u>-hiwalay	*n*ag*hi*hi<u>wa</u>-hiwalay	mag*hi*hi<u>wa</u>-hiwalay

Sentences:

Nag<u>kita</u>-<u>ki</u>ta' sina Shirley, Edmond at Alejandro.	*Shirley, Edmond and Alejandro saw one another.*
Nag<u>kahiwa</u>-hiwalay ang <u>gru</u>po.	*The group got separated from one another.*

mag- +rep2 [2]

POD: doer

to do something occasionally, at random, a little, a bit, now and then or here and there

root	meaning	root + affix	meaning
walis	*broom*	**magwalis-walis**	*to sweep a little (etc.)*
<u>la</u>kad	*walking*	**maglakad-lakad**	*to do a little walking (etc.)*
<u>i</u>sip	*mind*	**mag-isip-isip**	*to do a little thinking (etc.)*
<u>ha</u>nap	*something sought*	**maghanap-hanap**	*to do a little searching (etc.)*

Aspects:

basic form	completed	uncompleted	unstarted
maglakad-lakad	*n*aglakad-lakad	*n*ag*la*lakad-lakad	mag*la*lakad-lakad
mag-isip-isip	*n*ag-isip-isip	*n*ag-*i*isip-isip	mag-*i*isip-isip

Sentences:

Naglakad-lakad si Gloria.	*Gloria did a little walking.*
Nag-isip-isip si Gerard.	*Gerard did a little thinking.*

mag-...-an

POD: doer
to do something together, simultaneously or reciprocally

root	meaning	root + affix	meaning
sulat	*letter, writing*	magsulatan	*to write each other*
tulong	*help*	magtulungan	*to help each other*
tawa	*laughter*	magtawanan	*to laugh together*
halik	*kiss*	maghalikan	*to kiss each other*

kwento	story	magkwentuhan	to tell stories to each other, to swap stories
kanta	song	magkantahan	to sing together, to sing one after another

Aspects:

basic form	completed	uncompleted	unstarted
magtulungan	nagtulungan	nagtutulungan	magtutulungan
magkantahan	nagkantahan	nagkakantahan	magkakantahan

Sentences:

Nagtulungan sila.	They helped each other.
Nagkantahan sila.	They sang together. They sang one after another.

magka- [1]

POD: doer/none

to occur involuntarily or unexpectedly

root	meaning	root + affix	meaning
gulo	*commotion, mess*	magkagulo	*to become a mess*
salubong	*meeting, welcome*	magkasalubong	*to meet unexpectedly*

Aspects:

basic form	completed	uncompleted	unstarted
magkagulo	*n*agkagulo	*n*agk*a*kagulo	magk*a*kagulo
magkasalubong	*n*agkasalubong	*n*agk*a*ka-salubong	magk*a*ka-salubong

Sentences:

Nagkagulo.	*A commotion broke out.* *Chaos broke out.*
Nagkagulo ang mga raliyista.	*The protesters fell into chaos.* *The protesters became unruly.*
Nagkasalubong sina Chris at Tom.	*Chris and Tom bumped into each other.*

Note: **Magka-** and **magkaroon ng** mean the same thing.

Nagkagulo.	A commotion broke out.
Nagkaroon ng gulo.	Chaos broke out.

magka- [2]

POD: doer

to come to have or possess

root	meaning	root + affix	meaning
kotse	car	magkakotse	to get a car
trabaho	work	magkatrabaho	to get a job
sakit	illness	magkasakit	to get ill

Aspects:

basic form	completed	uncompleted	unstarted
magkakotse	nagkakotse	nagkakakotse	magkakakotse
magkasakit	nagkasakit	nagkakasakit	magkakasakit

Sentences:

Nagkakotse si Rose.	Rose got a car.
Nagkasakit si John.	John got ill.

Note: **Magka-** and **magkaroon ng** mean the same thing.

magkatra<u>ba</u>ho magkaroon ng tra<u>ba</u>ho	*to get a job*

magka- [3]

POD: doer
to manage to perform a reciprocal action

root	meaning	root + affix	meaning
<u>u</u>sap	*talking*	mag<u>kau</u>sap	*to manage to talk to each other*
bati'	*reconciled*	mag<u>ka</u>bati'	*to manage to reconcile, to manage to patch things up*

Aspects:

basic form	completed	uncompleted	unstarted
mag<u>kau</u>sap	*n*ag<u>kau</u>sap	*n*ag*ka*<u>kau</u>sap	mag*ka*<u>kau</u>sap
mag<u>ka</u>bati'	*n*ag<u>ka</u>bati'	*n*ag*ka*<u>ka</u>bati'	mag*ka*<u>ka</u>bati'

Sentences:

| Nagkausap sila. | *They managed to talk to each other.* |
| Nagkabati' sina John at Mike. | *John and Mike managed to patch things up.* |

magka- +rep2

POD: doer

to attain a certain state thoroughly

root	meaning	root + affix	meaning
basag	*a crack*	magkabasag-basag	*to get thoroughly broken*
sira'	*damage*	magkasira-sira'	*to get thoroughly damaged*
hiwalay	*separated*	magkahiwa-hiwalay	*to get thoroughly separated from one another*
halo'	*mixing*	magkahalu-halo'	*to get thoroughly mixed together, to get jumbled up*

Aspects:

basic form	completed	uncompleted	unstarted
magkahiwa-hiwalay	nagkahiwa-hiwalay	nagkakahiwa-hiwalay	magkakahiwa-hiwalay
magkahalu-halo'	nagkahalu-halo'	nagkakahalu-halo'	magkakahalu-halo'

Sentences:

Nagkahiwa-hiwalay ang grupo.	*The group got totally separated from one another.*
Nagkahalu-halo' ang mga papel.	*The papers got all mixed up together.*

magkanda-

POD: doer
to occur accidentally or involuntarily as a result of something and involving three or more doers

root	meaning	root + affix	meaning
hulog	*falling*	magkandahulog	*to fall accidentally (as a result)*
sira'	*damage*	magkandasira'	*to get damaged (as a result)*
wala'	*nothing*	magkandawala'	*to get lost (as a result)*

Aspects:

basic form	completed	uncompleted	unstarted
magkanda- hulog	nagkanda- hulog	nagkakanda- hulog	magkakanda- hulog
magkandasira'	nagkandasira'	nagkakanda- sira'	magkakanda- sira'

Sentences:

Nagkandahulog ang mga pinggan (dahil sa lindol).	*The dishes fell (to the floor) (because of the earthquake).*
Nagkandasira' ang mga computer (dahil sa kidlat).	*The computers got damaged (because of lightning).*

magma-

POD: doer

to pretend to be someone you are not; or, to assume a certain quality

root	meaning	root + affix	meaning
dunong	*knowledge*	magmarunong	*to pretend to be smart*
galing	*skill*	magmagaling	*to pretend to be clever*
linis	*cleanliness*	magmalinis	*to pretend to be innocent*
dali'	*quickness*	magmadali'	*to hurry*

Aspects:

basic form	completed	uncompleted	unstarted
magmarunong	*n*agmarunong	*n*ag*ma*-marunong	mag*ma*-marunong
magmadali'	*n*agmadali'	*n*ag*ma*madali'	mag*ma*madali'

Sentences:

Nag*ma*marunong si Maria.	*Maria is pretending to be smart.* *Maria thinks she knows everything.*
Nag*ma*madali' si Jay.	*Jay is hurrying.* *Jay is in a hurry.*

magpa-

POD: doer
to let, make or have someone do something; or,
to enable someone to do something

root	meaning	root + affix	meaning
laba	*washing of clothes*	**magpalaba**	*to have someone do the laundry*
pin<u>tu</u>ra	*paint*	**magpapin<u>tu</u>ra**	*to have someone paint something*

gupit	haircut, the way something is cut	magpagupit	to get a haircut
kain	eating	magpakain	to feed, to let someone or an animal eat
tulog	sleep	magpatulog	to put to bed, to knock out

Aspects:

basic form	completed	uncompleted	unstarted
magpagupit	nagpagupit	nagpapagupit	magpapagupit
magpatulog	nagpatulog	nagpapatulog	magpapatulog

Sentences:

Nagpagupit si Paul.	Paul got a haircut.
Nagpatulog si Jen ng bata'.	Jen put a/the child to bed.

Note:

The person permitted or asked to perform the action is generally expressed as—
- a Sa phrase (p. 70), if the underlying verb can take an object, or
- a Ng phrase (p. 70), if the underlying verb cannot take an object.

Examples:

magpa- verb	meaning	underlying verb
magpal<u>u</u>to'	*to have someone cook*	*Cook* can take an object. That is, someone can cook something, for example, adobo.
magpat<u>u</u>log	*to make someone sleep*	*Sleep* cannot take an object. That is, someone cannot "sleep" something.

Thus:

Nagpal<u>u</u>to' siya (ng a<u>d</u>obo) *sa* *kat<u>u</u>long*.	*He/she had **the maid** cook (adobo).*
Nagpat<u>u</u>log siya *ng* *b<u>a</u>ta'*.	*He/she put **a/the child** to bed.*

BUT: If the **magpa-** verb is used as a noun and the underlying verb cannot take an object, the person permitted or asked to perform the action is expressed as—
- a Sa phrase, if it is a personal name* or a personal pronoun,
- or else, either a Ng phrase or a Sa phrase.

Siya ang nagpat<u>u</u>log *kay John*.	*He/she was the one who put **John** to bed.*
Siya ang nagpat<u>u</u>log *sa kanila*.	*He/she was the one who put **them** to bed.*

Siya ang nagpa<u>tu</u>log *ng* <u>ba</u>ta'.	*He/she was the one who put a/the child to bed.*
Siya ang nagpa<u>tu</u>log *sa* <u>ba</u>ta'.	*He/she was the one who put **the** child to bed.*

* Personal names are names that refer to specific persons, animals, cartoon characters or anything with a personality.

See also:

- Verbs, adjectives etc. used as nouns (p. 101)
- Verbs used as nouns and their objects (p. 102)
- Ng personal pronouns (p. 58)
- Sa personal pronouns (p. 63)

magpaka-

POD: doer
to strive to be or do something

root	meaning	root + affix	meaning
bait	*kindness*	**magpakabait**	*to strive to be good*
totoo	*true*	**magpakatotoo**	*to strive to be true or honest*

Aspects:

basic form	completed	uncompleted	unstarted
magpakabait	*n*agpakabait	*n*ag*pa*pakabait	mag*pa*pakabait
magpakatotoo	*n*agpakatotoo	*n*ag*pa*paka-totoo	mag*pa*paka-totoo

Sentences:

Mag*pa*pakabait ako.	I'll try to be good. I'll try to behave myself.
Nagpakatotoo si Mark.	Mark strove to be authentic (e.g. he spoke his mind).

magsi-, magsipag-

POD: doer
to perform a collective action or an action involving three or more doers

root	meaning	root + affix	meaning
kain	eating	magsikain	to (all) eat
tulog	sleep	magsitulog	to (all) sleep
lakad	walking	magsipaglakad	to (all) walk
linis	cleaning	magsipaglinis	to (all) clean

Aspects:

basic form	completed	uncompleted	unstarted
magsi**kain**	*n*agsi**kain**	*n*ag*si*si**kain**	magsi*si*ka**in**
magsi**tulog**	*n*agsi**tulog**	*n*ag*si*si**tulog**	magsi*si*tu**log**

Sentences:

Nagsi**kain** sila.	*They all ate.*
Nagsi**tulog** sila.	*They all slept.*

maka- [1], makapag-, makapang-

POD: doer

to be able to do something

root	meaning	root + affix	meaning
kain	*eating*	maka**kain**	*to be able to eat*
kita'	*seeing*	maka**kita'**	*to be able to see*
tulog	*sleep*	maka**tulog**	*to be able to sleep*
rinig	*something heard*	maka**rinig**	*to be able to hear*
luto'	*cooking, cuisine*	makapag**luto'**	*to be able to cook*

166 *Essential Tagalog Grammar*

aral	lesson, studying	makapag-aral	to be able to study
daya'	deceit	makapandaya'	to be able to cheat

Aspects:

basic form	completed	uncompleted	unstarted
makakain	nakakain	nakakakain nakakakain	makakakain makakakain
makatulog	nakatulog	nakakatulog nakatutulog	makakatulog makatutulog

Sentences:

Nakakain si Jon.	Jon was able to eat.
Nakatulog si Bay.	Bay was able to sleep.

maka- [2]

POD: doer
to do something unintentionally or accidentally

root	meaning	root + affix	meaning
kain	eating	makakain	to eat unintentionally
bangga'	colliding	makabangga'	to bump or collide (with)

tulog	sleep	makatulog	to fall asleep unintentionally
basag	a crack	makabasag	to crack or break (something) accidentally
kita'	seeing	makakita'	to see unintentionally
patay	dead	makapatay	to kill unintentionally
hanap	finding, something sought	makahanap	to find unintentionally

Aspects:

basic form	completed	uncompleted	unstarted
makatulog	nakatulog	nakakatulog nakatutulog	makakatulog makatutulog
makahanap	nakahanap	nakakahanap nakahahanap	makakahanap makahahanap

Sentences:

Nakakain si Jun ng buto.	Jun accidentally swallowed (ate) a pit.
Nakahanap sila ng ginto'.	They found gold (by chance).

maka- [3]

POD: doer

to feel or experience something

root	meaning	root + affix	meaning
halata'	*obvious, noticeable*	makahalata'	*to notice*
damdam	*feeling*	makaramdam	*to feel*

Aspects:

basic form	completed	uncompleted	unstarted
makahalata'	*n*akahalata'	*n*aka*a*kahalata' *n*aka*ha*halata'	ma*ka*kahalata' maka*ha*halata'
makaramdam	*n*akaramdam	*n*aka*ka*karamdam *n*aka*ra*ramdam	ma*ka*karamdam maka*ra*ramdam

Sentences:

Nakahalata' sila.	*They noticed.*
Walang nakahalata'.	*Nobody noticed.*
Nakaramdam si Lex ng lindol.	*Lex felt an earthquake.*

makapag-, makapang-

See: maka- [1], makapag-, makapang- (p. 166)

maki- [1]

POD: doer

to join in an act

root	meaning	root + affix	meaning
kain	eating	makikain	to join in eating
kanta	song, singing	makikanta	to join in singing
sakay	passenger, load, riding	makisakay	to get a ride (to join in riding a vehicle)

Aspects:

basic form	completed	uncompleted	unstarted
makikain	nakikain	nakikikain	makikikain
makisakay	nakisakay	nakikisakay	makikisakay

Sentences:

Nakikain sa kanila si Mimi.	Mimi joined them in eating.
Nakisakay kay Madeline si Arthur.	Arthur asked Madeline for a ride.

maki- [2]

POD: doer

to do something involving someone else's possessions or personal space with their permission

root	meaning	root + affix	meaning
daan	*path, road*	**makiraan**	*to pass through with someone's permission*
tawag	*call*	**makitawag**	*to use someone's phone with his or her permission*

Aspects:

basic form	completed	uncompleted	unstarted
makiraan	**n**akiraan	**n**a**ki**kiraan	ma**ki**kiraan
makitawag	**n**akitawag	**n**a**ki**kitawag	ma**ki**kitawag

Sentences:

Nakiraan si Marlene sa kapitbahay.	*Marlene passed through a neighbor's yard (with permission).*
Nakitawag si Martin sa kapitbahay.	*Martin used a neighbor's phone (with permission).*

makipag-

POD: doer

to do something with someone

root	meaning	root + affix	meaning
usap	*talking*	makipag-usap	*to speak with*
kita'	*seeing*	makipagkita'	*to meet*
away	*fight*	makipag-away	*to quarrel or fight with*
hiwalay	*separated*	makipaghiwalay	*to separate from*

Aspects:

basic form	completed	uncompleted	unstarted
makipag-usap	*n*akipag-usap	*na*ki*kipag-usap	ma*ki*kipag-usap
makipag-away	*n*akipag-away	*na*ki*kipag-away	ma*ki*kipag-away

Sentences:

Nakipag-usap si Gay kay Lillian.	*Gay spoke with Lillian.*
Nakipag-away si Bing kay Bong.	*Bing fought with Bong.*

makipag-...-an

POD: doer

to do something with someone

root	meaning	root + affix	meaning
sagot	*answer*	makipag-sagutan	*to argue with*
tulak	*push, shove*	makipag-tulakan	*to push and shove together with other people*

Aspects:

basic form	completed	uncompleted	unstarted
makipag-sagutan	*n*akipag-sagutan	*n*a*ki*kipag-sagutan	ma*ki*kipag-sagutan
makipag-tulakan	*n*akipag-tulakan	*n*a*ki*kipag-tulakan	ma*ki*kipag-tulakan

Sentences:

Nakipagsagutan si Loy kay Doy.	*Loy argued with Doy.*
Nakipagtulakan si Michelle sa ibang fans.	*Michelle pushed and shoved against other fans.*

Verbs 173

mang- [1]

POD: doer

to do something (expresses various kinds of actions)

root	meaning	root + affix	meaning
anak	*child (son or daughter)*	manganak	*to give birth*
yari (not used on its own)	*happening*	mangyari	*to happen*
ngawit	*tiredness from prolonged standing, kneeling etc.*	mangawit	*to get tired from standing, kneeling etc.*

Aspects:

basic form	completed	uncompleted	unstarted
manganak	*n*anganak	*nanga*nganak	ma*nga*nganak
mangyari	*n*angyari	*n*ang*ya*yari	mang*ya*yari

Sentences:

Nanganak si Tagpi' kahapon.	*Tagpi gave birth yesterday.*
Nangyari ang aksidente kahapon.	*The accident happened yesterday.*

mang- [2]

POD: doer

to perform an action directed toward multiple objects; or,
to do something repeatedly, habitually or professionally

root	meaning	root + affix	meaning
bili	*buying*	mamili	*to go shopping*
huli	*catching*	manghuli	*to catch (many birds, rats etc.)*
pitas	*picking*	mamitas	*to pick (many apples, cherries etc.)*
kahoy	*wood*	mangahoy	*to gather wood*
gamot	*medicine*	manggamot	*to practise medicine*
kain	*eating*	mangain	*to kill and eat habitually*
kagat	*bite*	mangagat	*to bite habitually*

Aspects:

basic form	completed	uncompleted	unstarted
mamili	namili	namimili	mamimili
mangagat	nangagat	nangangagat	mangangagat

Sentences:

Namili ng re<u>ga</u>lo si Dora.	*Dora went shopping for gifts.*
Na<u>ngangai</u>n ng <u>ta</u>o ang <u>ti</u>gre.	*Tigers eat humans.* *The tiger eats humans.*
Hindi' na<u>nga</u>ngagat ang <u>a</u>so.	*The dog doesn't bite.*

mang- [3]

POD: doer

to do something harmful or destructive deliberately

root	meaning	root + affix	meaning
a<u>ba</u>la	*bothering*	**mang-a<u>ba</u>la**	*to bother*
<u>da</u>ya'	*deceit*	**man<u>da</u>ya'**	*to cheat*
gulo	*commotion, mess*	**manggulo**	*to create disorder, to cause trouble or confusion*
sakit	*pain*	**manakit**	*to hurt*
<u>ga</u>ntso	*hook*	**mang<u>ga</u>ntso**	*to deceive with a confidence trick*

Aspects:

basic form	completed	uncompleted	unstarted
man*daya*'	*n*an*daya*'	*n*an*da*daya'	man*da*daya'
manggulo	*n*anggulo	*n*ang*gu*gulo	mangg*u*gulo

Sentences:

Nan*daya*' si Dan.	*Dan cheated.*
Nanggugulo sila.	*They're causing trouble (or confusion).*

mang- [4]

POD: doer
to do a recreational activity

root	meaning	root + affix	meaning
ka*bay*o	*horse*	manga*bay*o	*to go horseback riding*
bangka'	*boat*	mamangka'	*to go boating*
pasyal	*visiting*	mamasyal	*to visit and take a walk around, to go for a walk in*

Aspects:

basic form	completed	uncompleted	unstarted
manga<u>bay</u>o	<i>n</i>anga<u>bay</u>o	<i>n</i>a<i>ng</i>a<i>ng</i>a<u>bay</u>o	ma<i>ng</i>a<i>ng</i>a<u>bay</u>o
mamasyal	<i>n</i>amasyal	<i>n</i>a<i>ma</i>masyal	ma<i>ma</i>masyal

Sentences:

Nangabayo si Erik.	*Erik went horseback riding.*
Namasyal si Samantha sa Rizal Park.	*Samantha went for a walk in Rizal Park.*

mang- [5]

POD: doer
to become something partially or temporarily

root	meaning	root + affix	meaning
pula	*red*	mamula	*to redden, to blush*
itim	*black*	mangitim	*to blacken, to become dark*
tigas	*hardness*	manigas	*to become hard, to become paralyzed with fear*

Aspects:

basic form	completed	uncompleted	unstarted
mamula	*n*amula	*n*a*mu*mula	ma*mu*mula
manigas	*n*anigas	*n*a*ni*nigas	ma*ni*nigas

Sentences:

Namula si Cesar.	*Cesar blushed.*
Nanigas si Consuelo sa <u>ta</u>kot.	*Consuelo froze in fear.*

mapa- [1]

POD: doer
to do something involuntarily

root	meaning	root + affix	meaning
sigaw	*shout*	mapasigaw	*to shout unintentionally*
iyak	*cry*	mapaiyak	*to cry unintentionally*
hiya'	*shame*	mapahiya'	*to be embarrassed, to be humiliated*
tingin	*look*	mapatingin	*to look unintentionally*

Aspects:

basic form	completed	uncompleted	unstarted
mapaiyak	*n*apaiyak	*n*a*pa*paiyak *n*apa*i*iyak	ma*pa*paiyak mapa*i*iyak
mapahiya'	*n*apahiya'	*n*a*pa*pahiya' *n*apa*hi*hiya'	ma*pa*pahiya' mapa*hi*hiya'

Sentences:

Napaiyak si Pong.	*Pong broke down and cried.*
Napahiya' si Dingdong.	*Dingdong was humiliated.*

mapa- [2]

POD: object
to be able to let, make or have someone do something; or,
to be able to cause something to become something

root	meaning	root + affix	meaning
pasok	*entry*	**mapapa**sok	*to be able to get someone to enter*
kain	*eating*	**mapaka**in	*to be able to get someone to eat, to be able to feed*

kintab	*gloss, shine*	mapakintab	*to be able to make something shine (e.g. by polishing it)*
tulog	*sleep*	mapatulog	*to be able to get someone to sleep, to be able to knock out*

Aspects:

basic form	completed	uncompleted	unstarted
mapatulog	napatulog	napapatulog napatutulog	mapapatulog mapatutulog
mapakain	napakain	napapakain napakakain	mapapakain mapakakain

Sentences:

Napatulog ni Mia ang baby.	*Mia was able to get the baby to sleep.* *Mia was able to let the baby sleep.*
Napakain ni Mark ang aso.	*Mark was able to get the dog to eat.* *Mark was able to feed the dog.*

pa-...-an [1]

POD: object

to let, make or have someone do something

root	meaning	root + affix	meaning
bukas	*open*	pabuksan	*to have someone open something*
palit	*changing*	papalitan	*to have replaced*
hugas	*washing*	pahugasan	*to have someone wash something*
laba	*washing of clothes*	palabhan	*to have someone wash clothes*
pinta	*paint*	papintahan	*to have someone paint something*

Aspects:

basic form	completed	uncompleted	unstarted
papintahan	pi*na*pintahan	*pina*papintahan pina*pi*pintahan	*pa*papintahan pa*pi*pintahan
pabuksan	pi*na*buksan	*pina*pabuksan pina*bu*buksan	*pa*pabuksan pa*bu*buksan

Sentences:

Pinapintahan ni Fred ang dingding.	Fred had the wall painted. Lit. "Had painted by Fred the wall."
Pinapintahan ni Fred kay John ang dingding.	Fred had John paint the wall. Lit. "Had painted by Fred by John the wall."*
Pinabuksan ni Mildred ang box.	Mildred had the box opened.

* First "by..." – permitter/causer of action; Ng phrase (p. 70)
Second "by..." – person permitted or asked to perform the action; Sa phrase (p. 70)

pa-...-an [2]

POD: direction
to let, make or have someone do something in the (physical or psychological) direction of

root	meaning	root + affix	meaning
sulat	letter, writing	pasulatan	to have someone write someone
lagay	putting	palagyan	to have someone put something somewhere
bigay	giving	pabigyan	to have someone give something to someone

tingin	*look*	patingnan	*to have someone look at something*
<u>ba</u>yad	*payment*	pab<u>a</u>yaran	*to have someone pay something*

Aspects:

basic form	completed	uncompleted	unstarted
patingnan	p*in*atingnan	p*ina*patingnan p*ina*t*i*tingnan	*pa*patingnan pat*i*tingnan
palagyan	p*in*alagyan	p*ina*palagyan p*ina*l*a*lagyan	*pa*palagyan pal*a*lagyan

Sentences:

Pinatingnan ni Thelma sa vet ang p<u>u</u>sa'.	*Thelma had a vet look at the cat.* Lit. *Thelma had the cat looked at by a vet.*
Pinalagyan ni Maribel ng carpet ang sahig.	*Maribel had someone put a carpet on the floor.* *Maribel had the floor carpeted.*

pa-...-in

POD: object

to let, make or have someone do something; or,

to cause something to get bigger, faster etc.

root	meaning	root + affix	meaning
ganda	*beauty*	pagandahin	*to make someone or something more beautiful or attractive*
tulog	*sleep*	patulugin	*to let or make someone sleep, to knock out*
lakad	*walking*	palakarin	*to make someone or an animal walk*
kain	*eating*	pakainin	*to let or make someone or an animal eat*
tuyo'	*dry*	patuyuin	*to let something dry*
laki	*size*	palakihin	*to make something bigger*
bilis	*speed*	pabilisin	*to make something faster*

Aspects:

basic form	completed	uncompleted	unstarted
patu_lugin_	pi_n_atu_lug_	pi_na_patu_lug_ pi_n_a_tutu_lug_	_pa_patulu_gin_ patu_tu_tulu_gin_
palakihin	pi_n_alaki	pi_na_palaki pi_n_al_a_laki	_pa_palakihin pal_a_lakihin

Sentences:

Pinatu_lug_ ni Justine ang b_a_ta'.	*Justine put the child to bed.*
Pinalaki ni Dane ang picture.	*Dane enlarged the picture.*

pag-...-an [1], pang-...-an

POD: direction

to do something in the (physical or psychological) direction of

root	meaning	root + affix	meaning
higanti	*revenge*	**paghigantihan**	*to take revenge on*
hi_ma_sok	*meddling*	**panghima_su_kan**	*to meddle in*
t_a_wa	*laughter*	**pagtawanan**	*to laugh at*
s_a_bi	*something said*	**pagsab_i_han**	*to reprimand, to reproach, to admonish*

Aspects:

basic form	completed	uncompleted	unstarted
pagtawanan	pinagtawanan	pinapagtawanan pinagtatawanan	papagtawanan pagtatawanan
pagsabihan	pinagsabihan	pinapagsabihan pinagsasabihan	papagsabihan pagsasabihan

Sentences:

Pinagtawanan nila si Weng.	*They laughed at Weng.*
Pinagsabihan ng teacher si Robert.	*Robert was reprimanded by the teacher.*

pag-...-an [2]
POD: location
to do something in/on/at

root	meaning	root + affix	meaning
kain	*eating*	pagkainan	*to eat in/on/at*
luto'	*cooking, cuisine*	paglutuan	*to cook in/on/at*
lagay	*putting*	paglagyan	*to put in/on/at*
tulog	*sleep*	pagtulugan	*to sleep in/on/at*
bili	*buying*	pagbilhan	*to buy in/on/at*

Aspects:

basic form	completed	uncompleted	unstarted
pagka<u>i</u>nan	pi*n*agka<u>i</u>nan	pi*na*pagka<u>i</u>nan pi*n*ag<u>ka</u>ka<u>i</u>nan	*pa*pagka<u>i</u>nan pag<u>ka</u>ka<u>i</u>nan
pagbilhan	pi*n*agbilhan	pi*na*pagbilhan pi*n*ag<u>bi</u>bilhan	*pa*pagbilhan pag<u>bi</u>bilhan

Sentences:

Pinagka<u>i</u>nan ni Jenna ang bowl.	*Jenna ate from (in) the bowl.*
Pinagbilhan ni Monique ng computer ang tin<u>da</u>han.	*Monique bought a computer from (at) the store.*

pag-...-an [3]

POD: reference
to do something concerning something

root	meaning	root + affix	meaning
<u>u</u>sap	*talking*	**pag-u<u>sa</u>pan**	*to talk about*
<u>a</u>way	*quarrel, fight*	**pag-a<u>wa</u>yan**	*to quarrel about*
kasundo'	*on good terms with*	**pag<u>ka</u>sunduan**	*to be in agreement about*

Aspects:

basic form	completed	uncompleted	unstarted
pag-u<u>sa</u>pan	pi<i>n</i>ag-u<u>sa</u>pan	<i>pina</i>pag-u<u>sa</u>pan pi<i>n</i>ag-<u>u</u>u<u>sa</u>pan	<i>pa</i>pag-u<u>sa</u>pan pag-<u>u</u>u<u>sa</u>pan
pag-a<u>wa</u>yan	pi<i>n</i>ag-a<u>wa</u>yan	<i>pina</i>pag-a<u>wa</u>yan pi<i>n</i>ag-<u>a</u>a<u>wa</u>yan	<i>pa</i>pag-a<u>wa</u>yan pag-<u>a</u>a<u>wa</u>yan

Sentences:

Pinag-u<u>sa</u>pan nila ang kasal.	*They talked about the wedding.*
Pinag-a<u>wa</u>yan nila ang <u>pe</u>ra.	*They fought over the money.*

pag- +rep1-...-an [1]

POD: object
to do something repeatedly, continually, a lot, intensively or frequently;
or, to do something to multiple objects

root	meaning	root + affix	meaning
bukas	*open*	**pagbubuksan**	*to open repeatedly (etc.)*
balat	*skin*	**pagbabalatan**	*to peel (many things) (etc.)*

Aspects:

basic form	completed	uncompleted	unstarted
pagbu- buksan	pi*n*agbu- buksan	pi*n*ag*bu*bubuksan pi*na*pagbubuksan	pag*bu*bubuksan *pa*pagbubuksan
pagba- balatan	pi*n*agba- balatan	pi*n*ag*ba*babalatan pi*na*pagbabalatan	pag*ba*babalatan *pa*pagbabalatan

Sentences:

Pinagbubuksan ni Jing ang mga kahon.	*Jing opened the boxes (and there were many of them).*
Pinagbabalatan ni Maribel ang mga mangga.	*Maribel peeled the mangoes (and there were many of them).*

pag- +rep1-...-an [2]

POD: direction

to do something in the (physical or psychological) direction of, repeatedly, continually, a lot, intensively or frequently; or, to do something directed toward multiple objects

root	meaning	root + affix	meaning
ta̲pak	*footstep*	**pagta̲ta̲pa̲kan**	*to step on repeatedly (etc.)*
lagay	*something put*	**paglalagyan**	*to put in/on repeatedly (etc.)*

190 *Essential Tagalog Grammar*

Aspects:

basic form	completed	uncompleted	unstarted
pagta-tapakan	pinagta-tapakan	pinag*ta*tatapakan pi*na*pagtatapakan	pag*ta*tatapakan *pa*pagtatapakan
paglalagyan	pinagla-lagyan	pinag*la*lalagyan pi*na*paglalagyan	pag*la*lalagyan *pa*paglalagyan

Sentences:

Pinagtatapakan nila ang mga kahon.	*They stepped/stomped on the boxes (and there were many of them).*
Pinaglalagyan nila ng tape ang mga kahon.	*They put tape on the boxes (and there were many of them).*

pag- +rep1 +rep1-...-an [1]

POD: object

to do something to multiple objects repeatedly, continually, a lot, intensively or frequently

root	meaning	root + affix	meaning
bukas	*open*	pagbubu-buksan	*to open (several things) repeatedly (etc.)*
balat	*peel*	pagbaba-balatan	*to peel (several things) repeatedly (etc.)*

Aspects:

basic form	completed	uncompleted	unstarted
pagbubu-buksan	pinagbubu-buksan	pinagbububu-buksan *pinapagbubu-buksan*	pagbububu-buksan *papagbubu-buksan*
pagbaba-balatan	pinagbaba-balatan	pinagbababa-balatan *pinapagbaba-balatan*	pagbababa-balatan *papagbaba-balatan*

Sentences:

Pinag<u>bu</u>bubuksan ni Jing ang mga kahon.	*Jing opened the boxes (repeatedly and there were many of them).*
Pinag<u>ba</u>babalatan ni Maribel ang mga mangga.	*Maribel peeled the mangoes (repeatedly and there were many of them).*

pag- +rep1 +rep1-...-an [2]

POD: direction

to do something directed toward multiple objects repeatedly, continually, a lot, intensively or frequently

root	meaning	root + affix	meaning
t<u>a</u>pak	*footstep*	**pagt<u>a</u>tat<u>a</u>pakan**	*to step on (several things) repeatedly (etc.)*
lagay	*something put*	**pagl<u>a</u>lalagyan**	*to put in/on (several things) repeatedly (etc.)*

Aspects:

basic form	completed	uncompleted	unstarted
pagtata- tapakan	pinagtata- tapakan	pinagtatata- tapakan pinapagtata- tapakan	pagtatata- tapakan papagtata- tapakan
paglalalagyan	pinaglala- lagyan	pinaglalala- lagyan pinapaglala- lagyan	paglalala- lagyan papaglala- lagyan

Sentences:

Pinagtatatapakan nila ang mga kahon.	*They stepped/stomped on the boxes (repeatedly and there were many of them).*
Pinaglalalagyan nila ng tape ang mga kahon.	*They put tape on the boxes (repeatedly and there were many of them).*

pag-...-in [1]

POD: object (person, animal or thing permitted or asked to perform the action)

to make someone do something

root	meaning	root + affix	meaning
luto'	cooking, cuisine	paglutuin	to make someone cook
linis	cleaning	paglinisin	to make someone clean

Aspects:

basic form	completed	uncompleted	unstarted
paglutuin	pinagluto'	pinapagluto' pinagluluto'	papaglutuin paglulutuin
paglinisin	pinaglinis	pinapaglinis pinaglilinis	papaglinisin paglilinisin

Sentences:

Pinagluto' ni Helen si Melanie.	Helen made Melanie cook.
Pinaglinis ni Maribel si Jing ng bahay.	Maribel made Jing clean the house.

pag-...-in [2]

POD: object

to put two things together or closer to each other

root	meaning	root + affix	meaning
sama	*joining, including*	pagsamahin	*to put together*
dugtong	*joining*	pagdugtungin	*to join together*
dikit	*sticking together*	pagdikitin	*to stick or paste together*
lapit	*nearness*	paglapitin	*to put near each other*

Aspects:

basic form	completed	uncompleted	unstarted
pagsamahin	pi*na*gsama	*pina*pagsama pi*nagsa*sama	*pa*pagsamahin pags*a*samahin
pagdikitin	pi*na*gdikit	*pina*pagdikit pi*nagdi*dikit	*pa*pagdikitin pag*di*dikitin

Sentences:

Pinagsama nila ang mga picture.	*They put the pictures together.*
Pinagdikit nila ang mga papel.	*They stuck the papers together.*

pag- +rep1-...-in

POD: object

to do something repeatedly, continually, a lot, intensively or frequently; or, to do something involving multiple objects

root	meaning	root + affix	meaning
gupit	*cut*	paggugupitin	*to cut repeatedly (etc.)*
isip	*mind*	pag-iisipin	*to think about repeatedly (etc.)*

Aspects:

basic form	completed	uncompleted	unstarted
paggu-gupitin	pinaggugupit	pinaggugupit / pinapaggugupit	paggugupitin / papaggugupitin
pag-iisipin	pinag-iisip	pinag-iiisip / pinapag-iisip	pag-iiisipin / papag-iisipin

Sentences:

Pinaggugupit ni Luz ang mga papel.	*Luz cut the papers (and there were many of them).*
Pinag-iisip ni Marie ang mga problema.	*Marie thought about the problems (and there were many of them).*

pag- +rep1 +rep1-...-in

POD: object

to do something to multiple objects repeatedly, continually, a lot, intensively or frequently

root	meaning	root + affix	meaning
luto'	cooking, cuisine	paglululutuin	to cook (several things) intensively (etc.)
kain	eating	pagkakakainin	to eat (several things) intensively (etc.)
sulat	letter, writing	pagsususulatin	to write (several things) intensively (etc.)

Aspects:

basic form	completed	uncompleted	unstarted
paglulu-lutuin	pinaglulu-luto'	pinaglulululuto' pinapaglululuto'	paglulululutuin papaglululutuin
pagsusu-sulatin	pinagsusu-sulat	pinagsusususulat pinapagsusususulat	pagsusususulatin papagsusususulatin

Sentences:

Pinaglululuto' ni Gay ang mga patatas.	*Gay cooked the potatoes (intensively and there were many of them).*
Pinagsususulat ni Cris ang mga pangalan.	*Cris wrote the names (intensively and there were many of them).*

pag- +rep2-...-in

POD: object
to put three or more things together or closer to one another

root	meaning	root + affix	meaning
sama	*joining, including*	**pagsama-samahin**	*to put 3 or more things together*
dugtong	*joining*	**pagdugtung-dugtungin**	*to join 3 or more things together*
tabi	*side*	**pagtabi-tabihin**	*to put 3 or more things next to one another*

Aspects:

basic form	completed	uncompleted	unstarted
pagsama-samahin	pinagsama-sama	pinagsasama-sama pinapagsama-sama	pagsasama-samahin papagsama-samahin
pagtabi-tabihin	pinagtabi-tabi	pinagtatabi-tabi pinapagtabi-tabi	pagtatabi-tabihin papagtabi-tabihin

Sentences:

Pinagsama-sama nila ang mga picture.	*They put the (3 or more) pictures together.*
Pinagtabi-tabi nila ang mga lamesa.	*They put the (3 or more) tables next to one another.*

pang-...-an

See: **pag-...-an** [1], **pang-...-an** (p. 186)

papang-...-in

POD: object (person, animal or thing permitted or asked to perform the action)

to let, make or have someone do something

root	meaning	root + affix	meaning
nood	*watching*	papanoorin	*to let or make someone watch something*
ako'	*promise* (rarely used)	papangakuin	*to let or make someone promise something*

Aspects:

basic form	completed	uncompleted	unstarted
papanoorin	pinapanood	*pina*papanood *pinapa*panood	*pa*papanoorin papa*pa*noorin
papangakuin	pinapangako'	*pina*papangako' pinapa*pa*ngako'	*pa*papangakuin papa*pa*ngakuin

Sentences:

Pinapanood ni Tingting si Jacky ng TV.	*Tingting let/made Jacky watch television.*
Pinapangako' ni Theresa si Rowan na tumawag.	*Theresa made Rowan promise to call.*

(-)um- [1]

POD: doer

to do something (expresses various kinds of actions)

Note: (-)um- is placed before the first vowel of the root.

root	meaning	root + affix	meaning
kain	*eating*	kumain	*to eat*
takbo	*running*	tumakbo	*to run*
lakad	*walking*	lumakad	*to walk*
sulat	*writing, letter*	sumulat	*to write*
pasok	*entry*	pumasok	*to enter*
punta	*going*	pumunta	*to go*
alis	*departure*	umalis	*to leave*
dating	*arrival*	dumating	*to arrive*
upo'	*sitting*	umupo'	*to sit*
gawa'	*making*	gumawa'	*to make*
iyak	*crying*	umiyak	*to cry*
bili	*buying, buying price*	bumili	*to buy*
kanta	*song*	kumanta	*to sing*
inom	*drinking*	uminom	*to drink*

Aspects:

basic form	completed	uncompleted	unstarted
ku*ma*in	ku*ma*in	*k*u*ma*kain	*ka*kain
tumakbo	tumakbo	*t*u*ma*takbo	*ta*takbo

Sentences:

Ku*ma*in si Ping.	*Ping ate.*
Tumakbo si Yoli.	*Yoli ran.*

(-)um- [2]

POD: none
expresses natural phenomena
Note: **(-)um-** is placed before the first vowel of the root.

root	meaning	root + affix	meaning
ulan	*rain*	**umulan**	*to rain*
araw	*sun*	**um*a*raw**	*to be sunny*
bagyo	*typhoon*	**bumagyo**	*to have a typhoon, to storm*
kulog	*thunder*	**kumulog**	*to thunder*
lindol	*earthquake*	**lumindol**	*to have an earthquake*

Aspects:

basic form	completed	uncompleted	unstarted
umulan	umulan	um_uu_ulan	_uu_ulan
lumindol	lumindol	l_umi_lindol	_li_lindol

Sentences:

U<u>muu</u>lan.	*It's raining.*
Lumindol.	*There was an earthquake.*

(-)um- [3]

POD: doer

to become or get

Note: (-)um- is placed before the first vowel of the root.

root	meaning	root + affix	meaning
taba'	*fat* (noun)	tumaba'	*to get fat*
payat	*thin*	pumayat	*to get thin*
laki	*size*	lumaki	*to get big, to grow*
tanda'	*age, seniority in age*	tumanda'	*to get old*
galing	*skill*	gumaling	*to improve, to get better, to get well*

Aspects:

basic form	completed	uncompleted	unstarted
pumayat	pumayat	pu<u>ma</u>payat	<u>pa</u>payat
gumaling	gumaling	gu<u>ma</u>galing	<u>ga</u>galing

Sentences:

Pumayat si Gloria.	*Gloria lost weight.*
Gumaling si Manny.	*Manny got better (became healthy again or became more skillful).*

(-)um- +rep2

POD: doer
to do something occasionally, at random, a little, a bit, now and then or here and there
Note: (-)um- is placed before the first vowel of the root.

root	meaning	root + affix	meaning
inom	*drinking*	uminom-inom	*to drink a bit (etc.)*
<u>ka</u>in	*eating*	ku<u>ma</u>in-<u>ka</u>in	*to eat a bit (etc.)*
kanta	*song*	kumanta-kanta	*to sing a little (etc.)*

Aspects:

basic form	completed	uncompleted	unstarted
ku<u>ma</u>in-<u>ka</u>in	ku<u>ma</u>in-<u>ka</u>in	k u<u>ma</u><u>ka</u>in-<u>ka</u>in	<u>ka</u>kain-<u>ka</u>in
kumanta-kanta	kumanta-kanta	k u<u>ma</u>kanta-kanta	<u>ka</u>kanta-kanta

Sentences:

Ku<u>ma</u>in-<u>ka</u>in si Alfred.	*Alfred ate a little.*
Kumanta-kanta si Raphael.	*Raphael sang a little.*

Aspects

Overview

The aspect of a verb indicates whether the action has been started or not, and, if started, whether it has been completed or not.

completed aspect	action has been completed
uncompleted aspect	action has been started but not completed or action is habitual or is a general fact
unstarted aspect	action has not been started

Some verbs have a fourth aspect.

recently completed aspect	action has been completed just before the time of speaking or just before some other specified time

Examples:

The different forms of the verb **magl_uto'** *(to cook)* are given below:

aspect	sentence	meaning
completed	*Nagl_uto'* **ang ba_bae.**	*The woman* *cooked.*
	Nagl_uto' *na* **ang ba_bae.***	*The woman* *has cooked.* *The woman* *had cooked* *(when something happened).*
uncompleted	*Nagl_ul_uto'* **ang ba_bae.**	*The woman* *cooks (e.g.* *every day).* *The woman* *is cooking* *(e.g. right now).* *The woman* *was cooking* *(when something happened).*
unstarted	*Magl_ul_uto'* **ang ba_bae.**	*The woman* *will cook.* *The woman* *cooks (e.g.* *tomorrow).* *The woman* *is cooking* *(e.g. tomorrow).*

| recently completed | *Ka<u>lulu</u>to' lang* ng ba<u>bae</u>.** | *The woman **has just cooked**.* *The woman **had just cooked** (when something happened).* |

* The completed form followed by **na** (p. 345) means *has/had....*

** The recently completed form is followed by either **lang** (p. 362) or **pa lang** (p. 356).

The rules for indicating aspect depend on the verb affix.

Completed

Rules for indicating completed aspect:

if basic form starts with	rule	basic form	completed
• an affix starting with /m/	replace /m/ by /n/	*m*aglu<u>to</u>' *m*abigyan *m*aibigay*	*n*aglu<u>to</u>' *n*abigyan *n*aibigay*
• **um-**, or • a consonant followed by **-um-**	no change	ku<u>ma</u>in umalis	ku<u>ma</u>in umalis

* Usually, the /i/ in /mai-/ and /nai-/ may be deleted. Thus: **mabigay, nabigay**.

In cases not covered above:

if basic form starts with	rule	basic form	completed
• /l/, /r/, /w/ or /y/, or • i- followed by /l/, /r/, /w/ or /y/	• insert /ni/ before /l/, /r/, /w/ or /y/* • remove final -in/ -hin/-nin if present	lu<u>tu</u>an lasingin i<u>la</u>pit	*ni*lu<u>tu</u>an *ni*lasing i*ni*<u>la</u>pit*
• any other consonant, or • i- followed by any other consonant	• insert /in/ after first consonant • remove final -in/ -hin/-nin if present	sa<u>bi</u>han sa<u>bi</u>hin i<u>ta</u>pon	si*n*a<u>bi</u>han si*n*abi iti*n*apon*
• a vowel, or • i- followed by a vowel	• place /in/ at beginning of word • remove final -in/ -hin/-nin if present	alisan alisin iabot	i*n*alisan i*n*alis i*n*iabot**

* Alternative: Insert /in/ after /l/, /r/, /w/ or /y/. Thus: li*n*u<u>tu</u>an, li*n*asing, ili*n*apit.

** /i/ may be deleted from the completed form. Thus: *ni*<u>la</u>pit, ti*n*apon, i*n*abot.

Uncompleted

Rule: Take the completed form and repeat the first syllable of the root (rep1).

See also: Completed form (p. 208), Syllable repetition (p. 33), Sound changes when combining roots and affixes (p. 31)

basic form	completed	uncompleted
mag<u>lu</u>to'	*n*ag<u>lu</u>to'	*n*ag<u>lulu</u>to'
maibigay	*n*aibigay	*n*ai<u>bi</u>bigay
mabigay	*n*abigay	*n*a<u>bi</u>bigay
ku<u>ma</u>in	ku<u>ma</u>in	*k*u<u>ma</u>kain
umalis	umalis	um<u>a</u>alis
lu<u>tu</u>an	*ni*lu<u>tu</u>an	*ni*<u>lu</u>lu<u>tu</u>an
	*li*n<u>utu</u>an	*li*<u>nu</u>lu<u>tu</u>an
sa<u>bi</u>hin	si<u>na</u>bi	si<u>na</u>sabi
iabot	*in*iabot	*in*i<u>a</u>abot
	*in*abot	*in*<u>a</u>abot

Exception: In the case of a few affixes, a syllable of the affix is repeated instead of the first syllable of the root.

basic form	completed	uncompleted
maki<u>ka</u>in affix: **maki-**	*n*aki<u>ka</u>in	*n*a<u>ki</u>ki<u>ka</u>in
magpa<u>ka</u>in affix: **magpa-**	*n*agpa<u>ka</u>in	*n*ag<u>pa</u>pa<u>ka</u>in

magka<u>kot</u>se affix: **magka-**	*n*agka<u>kot</u>se	*n*ag*ka*ka<u>kot</u>se
magsi<u>ka</u>in affix: **magsi-**	*n*agsi<u>ka</u>in	*n*ag*si*si<u>ka</u>in
magsipagbasa affix: **magsipag-**	*n*agsipagbasa	*n*ag*si*sipagbasa

Alternative: In the case of a few prefixes containing a /ka/ or a /pa/, these syllables may be repeated instead of the first syllable of the root. This option is commonly used in spoken Tagalog.

basic form	completed	uncompleted (usually formal)	uncompleted (usually informal)
maka<u>ba</u>sa affix: **maka-**	*n*aka<u>ba</u>sa	*n*aka*ba*<u>ba</u>sa	*n*a*ka*ka<u>ba</u>sa
makapagbasa affix: **makapag-**	*n*akapagbasa	*n*akapag*ba*basa	*n*a*ka*kapagbasa
papuntahin affix: **pa-...-in**	*pin*apunta	*pin*a*pu*punta	*pi*na*papunta
pagba<u>wa</u>lan affix: **pag-...-an**	*pin*ag- ba<u>wa</u>lan	*pin*ag- *ba*ba<u>wa</u>lan	*pi*na*pag- ba<u>wa</u>lan
ipag<u>ba</u>wal affix: **ipag-**	i*pin*ag<u>ba</u>wal	i*pin*ag*ba*bawal	i*pi*na*pag<u>ba</u>wal

Unstarted

Rule: Take the basic form and repeat the first syllable of the root (rep1).

See also: Syllable repetition (p. 33), Sound changes when combining roots and affixes (p. 31)

Exception 1: If the affix is **(-)um-**, remove it.

basic form	unstarted
mag<u>lu</u>to'	mag*lu*<u>lu</u>to'
mai<u>bi</u>gay ma<u>bi</u>gay	mai*bi*<u>bi</u>gay ma*bi*<u>bi</u>gay
ku<u>ma</u>in	*ka*<u>ka</u>in
u<u>ma</u>lis	*a*alis
lu<u>tu</u>an	*lu*<u>lu</u>tuan
sa<u>bi</u>hin	*sa*sa<u>bi</u>hin
iabot	i*a*abot

Exception 2: In the case of a few affixes, a syllable of the affix is repeated instead of the first syllable of the root.

basic form	unstarted
maki<u>ka</u>in affix: **maki-**	ma*ki*ki<u>ka</u>in
mag*pa*<u>ka</u>in affix: **magpa-**	mag*pa*pa<u>ka</u>in

magka<u>ko</u>tse affix: **magka-**	mag<u>*ka*</u>ka<u>ko</u>tse
magsi<u>ka</u>in affix: **magsi-**	mag<u>*si*</u>si<u>ka</u>in
magsipagbasa affix: **magsipag-**	mag<u>*si*</u>sipagbasa

Alternative: In the case of a few prefixes containing a /**ka**/ or a /**pa**/, these syllables may be repeated instead of the first syllable of the root.
This option is commonly used in spoken Tagalog.

basic form	unstarted (usually formal)	unstarted (usually informal)
maka<u>ba</u>sa affix: **maka-**	maka<u>*ba*</u><u>ba</u>sa	ma<u>*ka*</u>ka<u>ba</u>sa
makapagbasa affix: **makapag-**	makapag<u>*ba*</u>basa	ma<u>*ka*</u>kapagbasa
papuntahin affix: **pa-...-in**	pa<u>*pu*</u>puntahin	<u>*pa*</u>papuntahin
pagba<u>wa</u>lan affix: **pag-....-an**	pag<u>*ba*</u>ba<u>wa</u>lan	<u>*pa*</u>pagba<u>wa</u>lan
ipag<u>ba</u>wal affix: **ipag-**	ipag<u>*ba*</u><u>ba</u>wal	i<u>*pa*</u>pagba<u>ba</u>wal

Summary

basic form	completed	uncompleted	unstarted
magluto'	nagluto'	nagluluto'	magluluto'
maibigay	naibigay	naibibigay	maibibigay
mabigay	nabigay	nabibigay	mabibigay
kumain	kumain	kumakain	kakain
umalis	umalis	umaalis	aalis
lutuan	nilutuan	nilulutuan	lulutuan
	linutuan	linulutuan	
sabihin	sinabi	sinasabi	sasabihin
iabot	iniabot	iniaabot	iaabot
	inabot	inaabot	

basic form	completed	uncompleted	unstarted
makikain	nakikain	nakikikain	makikikain
magpakain	nagpakain	nagpapakain	magpapakain
magkakotse	nagkakotse	nagkakakotse	magkakakotse
magsikain	nagsikain	nagsisikain	magsisikain
magsipagbasa	nagsipagbasa	nagsisipagbasa	magsisipagbasa

basic form	completed	uncompleted	unstarted
makabasa	nakabasa	nakababasa nakakabasa	makababasa makakabasa
makapag-basa	nakapagbasa	nakapagbabasa nakakapagbasa	makapagbabasa makakapagbasa
papuntahin	pinapunta	pinapupunta pinapapunta	papupuntahin papapuntahin
pagbawalan	pinagbawalan	pinagbabawalan pinapagbawalan	pagbabawalan papagbawalan
ipagbawal	ipinagbawal	ipinagbabawal ipinapagbawal	ipagbabawal ipapagbawal

Recently completed

Rules for indicating recently completed aspect:

affix	rule: remove affix, then add —	basic form	recently completed	recently completed (alternative)
(-)um- ma- mag-	• kaka- or • ka- +rep1*	lumapit mahulog magluto'	kakalapit kakahulog kakaluto'	kalalapit kahuhulog kaluluto'
mag-	• kakapag-, kapapag- or • kapag- +rep1	magluto'	kakapag- luto' kapapag- luto'	kapaglu- luto'

mang-	• <u>ka</u>kapang-, ka<u>pa</u>pang- or • kapang- +rep1	mang<u>ga</u>mit	<u>ka</u>kapang- gamit ka<u>pa</u>pang- gamit	kapang<u>ga</u>- gamit
magpa-	• <u>ka</u>kapa-, ka<u>pa</u>pa-, kapag<u>pa</u>pa- or • kapa- +rep1	magpa<u>lu</u>to'	<u>ka</u>kapa<u>lu</u>to' ka<u>pa</u>pa<u>lu</u>to' kapag<u>pa</u>pa- <u>lu</u>to'	kapa<u>lulu</u>to'

* See also: Syllable repetition (p. 33)

Note:

1. Verbs in the recently completed form are followed by either **lang** (p. 362) or **pa lang** (p. 356).

<u>Kaka</u>kain *lang* ni Chris.	*Chris has just eaten.*
<u>Kaka</u>kain *pa lang* ni Chris.	*Chris just ate.*

2. The doer of the action is expressed as a Ng phrase (p. 70).

<u>Kaka</u>kain lang *ni Chris.*	*Chris has just eaten.* *Chris just ate.*
<u>Kaka</u>kain lang *nila.*	*They have just eaten.* *They just ate.*

3. The object of the action may be expressed as a Ng phrase (indefinite/definite) or a Sa phrase (p. 70) (definite).

Kakakain lang ni Chris *ng* mangga.	*Chris just ate a/the mango.*
Kakakain lang ni Chris *sa* mangga.	*Chris just ate the mango.*

Intensive recently completed

Verbs in the intensive recently completed form express extremely recent actions *("just this minute")*.

How to form:
recently completed form +rep2

Either of the following are usually repeated:
* the first two syllables of the root (except if preceded by /**pang**/)
* /**pag**/, /**pang**/ or /**pa**/ and the the first syllable of the root

recently completed	intensive recently completed
ka**ka**la**pit**	ka**ka**la*pit*-la**pit**
ka**la**la**pit**	ka**la**la*pit*-la**pit**
ka**lu**lu**to'**	ka**lu**lu*tu*-lu**to'**
ka**papag**lu**to'**	ka**papag**lu*tu*-lu**to'** ka**papag**lu-pag**lu**to'
ka**papang**ga**mit**	ka**papang**ga-pang**ga**mit
ka**papa**lu**to'**	ka**papa**lu*tu*-lu**to'** ka**papa**lu-pa**lu**to'

See also:

- Recently completed form (p. 215)
- Syllable repetition (p. 33)
- Sound changes when combining roots and affixes (p. 31)

Irregular verbs

Some roots change forms when an affix is added to them. For example, a particular root may lose a vowel when **-an** or **-in** is added to it.

These changes are different from the usual sound changes that occur when combining roots and affixes. See also: Sound changes when combining roots and affixes (p. 31)

Below is a list of the most common irregular verbs.

The roots and root-affix combinations may have more meanings than the ones given here.

root	meaning	root + affix	meaning
ala<u>a</u>la	*memory*	alala<u>ha</u>nin	*to keep in mind, to take into account*
bigay	*something given*	bigyan	*to give to*
bili	*buying, buying price*	bilhan	*to buy for (to buy someone)*
		bilhin	*to buy*

bukas	*open*	buksan	*to open*
dala	*something brought*	dalhan	*to bring for (to bring someone)*
		dalhin	*to bring*
dating	*arrival*	datnan	*to catch or find on arrival*
gawa'*	*something made*	gawan	*to make for (to make someone)*
		gawin	*to make, to do*
hingi'	*asking (for something)*	hingan	*to ask from*
		hingin	*to ask for*
ihip	*blowing*	hipan	*to blow on*
iwan	*leaving*	iwan iwanan	*to leave, to leave something for*
kinig	*hearing*	pakinggan	*to listen to*
kuha'	*getting*	kunan	*to get or take for*
		kunin	*to get or take*
lagay	*putting*	lagyan	*to put something in/on/at*
sakay	*riding, a ride*	sakyan	*to ride*
sakit	*pain*	saktan	*to hurt*

sunod	following	sundan	to follow (somewhere)
		sundin	to obey
takip	lid	takpan	to cover
tikim	tasting	tikman	to taste
tingin	look	tingnan	to look at
tira	living, residing	tirhan	to live in

Commands, requests and wishes

Commands

Commands are formed in the following ways:

1. basic form + ka/kayo/mo/ninyo

| Kumain ka. | Eat.
Lit. You eat. |
| Kainin mo ito. | Eat this.
Lit. This is to be eaten by you. |

2. basic form in the POD (p. 35)
The News (p. 35) is emphasized in this construction.

| Ito ang kainin mo. | Eat this. (e.g. not that)
Lit. The one to be eaten by you is this. |

Ang cake ang ka<u>i</u>nin mo.	*Eat the cake. (e.g. not the ice cream)* Lit. *The one to be eaten by you is the cake.*
Ikaw ang ku<u>ma</u>in.	*You eat. (e.g. not me)* Lit. *The one to eat is you.*

3. verb root (+ **na**)

Alis!	*Leave!*
Alis na!	*Leave now!*

See also:

* Ang personal pronouns (p. 53)
* Ng personal pronouns (p. 58)
* Verbs, adjectives etc. used as nouns (p. 101)

Requests

Requests are formed in the following ways:

1. **pa-** + root (+ Ng phrase (p. 70))

Pahiram.	*Can I borrow it?* Lit. *Could you let me borrow it.*
Pahiram ng ballpen.	*Can I borrow a pen?* Lit. *Could you let me borrow a pen.*

| Pahingi' ng scratch paper. | Can I have some scratch paper? Lit. Could you let me have/get some scratch paper. |
| Paabot ng isda'. | Could you pass the fish. |

2. paki- + root (+ Ng phrase)

| Pakiabot ng isda'. | Could you pass the fish. |
| Pakitanggal nito. | Could you remove this. |

3. paki-...-an + root (+ Ang phrase (p. 70) or Ng phrase)

Pakibuksan ang pinto'.*	Could you open the door.
Pakihugasan ang pinggan.	Could you do (wash) the dishes.
Pakilagyan ng check ang kahon.*	Could you put a check in the box.

* The roots are **bukas** and **lagay**. See also: Irregular verbs (p. 218)

Let's eat, go etc.

1. basic form + <u>tayo/natin</u>

| Kumain tayo. | Let's eat. Lit. We eat. |
| Kainin natin ito. | Let's eat this. Lit. This is to be eaten by us. |

2. basic form in the POD (p. 35)
The News (p. 35) is emphasized in this construction.

| Ito ang ka<u>i</u>nin <u>na</u>tin. | *Let's eat this. (e.g. not that)* Lit. *The one to be eaten by us is this.* |
| Ang cake ang ka<u>i</u>nin <u>na</u>tin. | *Let's eat the cake. (e.g. not the ice cream)* Lit. *The one to be eaten by us is the cake.* |

See also:

* Ang personal pronouns (p. 53)
* Ng personal pronouns (p. 58)
* Verbs, adjectives etc. used as nouns (p. 101)

I wish, I hope etc.

1. basic form + <u>sana</u>
I hope

| Ma<u>na</u>lo <u>sa</u>na si Pacquiao. <u>Sa</u>na ma<u>na</u>lo si Pacquiao. | *May Pacquiao win.* *I hope Pacquiao wins.* |

2. basic form in the POD (p. 35) + <u>sana</u>
I hope

| Si Pacquiao <u>sa</u>na ang ma<u>na</u>lo. | *I hope it's Pacquiao who wins.* |

3. basic form + **kaya'**
should perhaps

Ku<u>ma</u>in kaya' <u>ta</u>yo.	*Perhaps we should eat.*
Mag<u>lu</u>to' kaya' siya.	*Perhaps he/she should cook.*
Tingnan ko kaya'.	*Perhaps I should have a look.* *Lit. (It/They) should perhaps be looked at by me.*
Hug<u>a</u>san ko kaya' ang pinggan.	*Perhaps I should do (wash) the dishes.* *Lit. The dishes should perhaps be washed by me.*

4. basic form + **nga'**
why don't

Ku<u>ma</u>in nga' <u>ta</u>yo.	*Why don't we eat.*
Ta<u>wa</u>gan nga' <u>na</u>tin siya.	*Why don't we call him/her.*
Maghintay nga' sila.	*Why don't they wait.*

5. basic form + **siya/niya/sila/nila**
let him/her/them

Maghintay siya.	*Let him/her wait.*
Iyon ang ka<u>i</u>nin niya.	*Let him/her eat that.*

Maghintay sila.	*Let them wait.*
Iyon ang ka<u>i</u>nin nila.	*Let them eat that.*

See also:

- Ang personal pronouns (p. 53)
- Ng personal pronouns (p. 58)
- Verbs, adjectives etc. used as nouns (p. 101)

Huwag

Huwag is used to form a negative command, request or wish.

1. huwag ka/kayo/mo/ninyo -ng + basic form
don't
Note: The unstarted form (p. 212) of the verb may also be used.

Huwag kang kumain. Huwag kang kakain.	*Don't eat.*
Huwag mong kainin ito. Huwag mong kakainin ito.	*Don't eat this.*

2. huwag tayo/natin -ng + basic form
let's not

Huwag tayong kumain.	*Let's not eat.*
Huwag nating kainin ito.	*Let's not eat this.*

3. huwag sana -ng + basic form
I hope... not

Huwag sanang manalo si Pacquiao.	*I hope Pacquiao doesn't win.*

4. huwag kaya' -ng + basic form
perhaps... shouldn't

Huwag kaya' tayong kumain.	*Perhaps we shouldn't eat.*
Huwag kaya' siyang magluto'.	*Perhaps he/she shouldn't cook.*
Huwag ko kayang tingnan.	*Perhaps I shouldn't have a look.* Lit. *(It/They) perhaps shouldn't be looked at by me.*

Huwag can also be combined with an adjective instead of a verb, as in the following sentences:

5. huwag – *don't be*

Huwag kang maingay.	*Don't be noisy.*

6. huwag – *let's not be*

Huwag tayong maingay.	*Let's not be noisy.*

7. Huwag can also stand alone.

Huwag.	*Don't.* *Don't do that.* *Let's not do that.*

See also:

- Ang personal pronouns (p. 53)
- Ng personal pronouns (p. 58)
- **Na/-ng** (p. 34)

Repeated verbs and verb roots

A verb or a root expressing an action can be repeated to express intense, repeated or prolonged action. The two verbs or roots are linked by **nang**.

When roots are used, the POD (p. 35) is the doer of the action.

Examples:

Umiyak nang umiyak ang <u>ba</u>ta'.	*The child cried and cried.* *The child kept on crying.*
Tumakbo siya nang tumakbo.	*He/she ran and ran.*
Iyak nang iyak ang <u>ba</u>ta'.	*The child keeps on crying.*
Takbo nang takbo si Forrest.	*Forrest runs and runs.*
<u>Ka</u>in nang <u>ka</u>in ang <u>ba</u>ta'.	*The child keeps on eating.*

Verbs expressing mental states or perception

Below are examples of verbs expressing mental states or perception.
Na/-ng (p. 34) precedes what is being thought of, felt or perceived.

ma<u>ki</u>ta' *to see*	Na<u>ki</u>ta' ko*ng* na<u>tutu</u>log si Tom.	*I saw Tom sleeping.* Lit. *(It) was seen by me* *that Tom was sleeping.*
marinig *to hear*	Narinig ko*ng* kumanta si Tom.	*I heard Tom sing.* Lit. *(It) was heard by* *me that Tom sang.*
maamoy *to smell*	Naamoy ko*ng* na<u>susu</u>nog ang <u>ka</u>nin.	*I smelled the rice* *burning.*
maramdaman *to feel*	Naramdaman ko*ng* gumalaw si Tom.	*I felt Tom move.*
mabali<u>ta</u>an *to hear (news)*	Nabali<u>ta</u>an ko*ng* na<u>na</u>lo si Tom.	*I heard that Tom won.*
mapansin *to notice*	Napansin ko*ng* na<u>tutu</u>log si Tom.	*I noticed that Tom was* *sleeping*
madatnan *to find* *someone or* *something on* *arrival*	Nadatnan ko*ng* na<u>tutu</u>log si Tom.	*I found Tom sleeping* *when I arrived.*

maabutan to arrive in time to catch something	Naabutan kong natutulog si Tom.	I arrived in time to catch Tom sleeping.
malimutan to forget	Nalimutan kong natutulog si Tom.	I forgot that Tom was sleeping
maalala to remember	Naalala kong natutulog si Tom.	I remembered that Tom was sleeping
maniwala' to believe	Naniwala' akong babalik si Tom.	I believed that Tom would come back/return.
ituring to consider	Itinuring kong kaibigan si Tom.	I considered Tom a friend.

Basic forms used as nouns

In the following sentence patterns, the basic form is equivalent to *to do/go/eat/etc.* or *doing/going/eating/etc.* in English.

If the word preceding the basic form ends in a vowel or /n/, -ng may be added to it. See also: Na/-ng (p. 34)

Adjective + basic form

b<u>a</u>wal *(it's)* *prohibited*	B<u>a</u>wal maniga<u>ri</u>lyo.	*It's prohibited to smoke.* *Smoking is prohibited.*
madali' *(it's) easy*	Madali*ng* mag<u>lu</u>to'.	*It's easy to cook.* *Cooking is easy.*
ma<u>hi</u>rap *(it's) hard*	Ma<u>hi</u>rap mag<u>lu</u>to'.	*It's hard to cook.* *Cooking is hard.*
ma<u>gas</u>tos *(it's)* *expensive*	Ma<u>gas</u>tos mag-upgrade.	*It's expensive to upgrade.*
na<u>kaka</u>pagod *(it's) tiring*	Na<u>kaka</u>pagod tumakbo.	*It's tiring to run.*
na<u>kaka</u>takot *(it's)* *frightening,* *scary*	Na<u>kaka</u>takot mag- skydiving.	*It's frightening to skydive.* *Skydiving is scary.*
na<u>kaka</u>aliw *(it's) amusing*	Na<u>kaka</u>aliw pano<u>o</u>rin ang <u>pu</u>sa'.	*It's amusing to watch the cat.*

mahilig *fond of*	Mahilig magluto' si Mary.	*Mary is fond of* *cooking.*
marunong *knowledgeable* *about (to know* *how)*	Marunong magluto' ang babae.	*The woman knows how* *to cook.*
sanay *experienced at,* *used to*	Sanay magluto' si Fred.	*Fred is experienced at* *cooking.*
magaling *good at*	Magaling magluto' si Fred.	*Fred is good at cooking.*

In some cases, the basic form may be preceded by **ang**.

Bawal ang manigarilyo.	*It's prohibited to smoke.* *Smoking is prohibited.*

An adjective may also precede a basic form to express the way the action is characteristically performed by someone or something.

Mabilis tumakbo si Fred.	*Fred is a fast runner.* *Fred runs fast.*
Malakas kumain si Fred.	*Fred is a big eater.* Lit. *Fred eats strongly.*

Non-basic-form verb + basic form

Note: The non-basic-form verbs in the example sentences are in the completed form (p. 208).

su<u>bu</u>kan *to try*	Sinu<u>bu</u>kang mag- upgrade ni Fred.	*Fred tried to upgrade.*
mag<u>pla</u>no *to plan*	Nag<u>pla</u>no*ng* umalis si John.	*John planned to leave.*
mapi<u>li</u>tan *to be forced (by circumstances)*	Napi<u>li</u>tang umalis si John.	*John was forced to leave.*
mahiya' *to be embarrassed*	Nahiya*ng* magtanong si John.	*John was embarrassed to ask.*
si<u>pa</u>gin *to get motivated, to get in the mood*	Si<u>ni</u>pag mag-<u>a</u>ral si Fred.	*Fred got motivated to study.*
tamarin *to lose motivation, to not be in the mood*	Tinamad magtra<u>ba</u>ho si John.	*John lost his motivation to work.*

hintayin *to wait for*	**Hinintay umalis ni John si Mark.**	*John waited for Mark to leave.*
tulungan *to help*	**Tinulungang magluto' ni John si Mark.**	*John helped Mark (to) cook.*
pilitin *to force*	**Pinilit magluto' ni John si Mark.**	*John forced Mark to cook.*
payagan *to allow*	**Pinayagang magluto' ni John si Mark.**	*John allowed Mark to cook.*
hayaan, bayaan, pabayaan *to let, to leave (someone alone to do something)*	**Hinayaang mag-aral ni John si Mark.**	*John left Mark alone to study.* *John let Mark study.*

Maging

Maging means *to be* or *to become*.

POD: doer
Aspects: **naging** (completed), **nagiging** (uncompleted), **magiging** (unstarted)

Naging mayor siya.	*He/she became mayor.*
Nagiging popular siya.	*He/she's becoming popular.*
Magiging popular siya.	*He/she will become popular.*
Mahirap maging magulang.	*It's hard to be a parent.*

See also: POD (p. 35), Aspects (p. 206)

Roots used as verbs

Certain roots may be used as regular verbs.

mahal *loved*	**Mahal ko si Frederik.**	*I love Frederik.* Lit. *Frederik is loved by me.*
kilala *known (used to refer to persons)*	**Kilala ko si John.**	*I know John.* Lit. *John is known by me.*

alam	Alam ko ang pangalan	I know his/her name.
known (used to refer to things or ideas)	niya.	Lit. His/her name is known by me.
	Alam kong babalik si John.	I know that John will come back. Lit. John will come back, is known by me.

suot	Suot ko ang T-shirt.	I'm wearing the T-shirt. Lit. The T-shirt is worn by me.
worn		

dala	Dala ko ang laptop.	I brought the laptop. Lit. The laptop is brought by me.
brought, carried		

sabi	Sabi ko, nandito siya.	I said, he/she's here
said		

akala'	Akala' ko, nandito siya.	I thought (mistakenly) he/she was here.
thought (mistakenly)		

Pseudo-verbs

Overview

ayaw	don't like/want, wouldn't like/want
gusto	like, would like, want
kaya	can (do), could (do) (expressing ability)
pwede	can, could, may, might (expressing possibility or permission)
kailangan	need, ought (to), must, should (often connotes a self-imposed need or duty)
dapat	ought (to), must, should (often connotes a need or duty imposed by others or society)

Note:

1. Pseudo-verbs have no aspects (p. 206).

2. In written Tagalog and formal spoken Tagalog, the following alternatives can be used:
- for **gusto**: **ibig, nais**
- for **pwede**: **maaari'**

3. When used alone as adjectives:
- **kaya** means *feasible*
- **kailangan** means *necessary*
- **pwede** means *allowed/possible*

Using pseudo-verbs

Ayaw, gusto, kaya, kailangan

The doer is expressed as a Ng phrase (p. 70). The object may be expressed as an Ang phrase (p. 70) (definite) or a Ng phrase (indefinite).

Ayaw ni John ang kotse.	*John doesn't like/want the car.*
Gusto ni John ang kotse.	*John likes/wants the car.*
Kaya ni John ang trabaho.	*John can do the job.*
Kailangan ni John ang trabaho.	*John needs the job.*

Ayaw ni John ng kotse.	*John doesn't want a car.*
Gusto ni John ng kotse.	*John wants a car.*
Kailangan ni John ng kotse.	*John needs a car.*

Only for **ayaw**: The object may also be expressed as a Sa phrase (p. 70) (definite).

Ayaw ni John sa kotse.	*John doesn't like the car.*
Ayaw ni John sa teacher.	*John doesn't like the teacher.*
Ayaw ni John sa kanya.	*John doesn't like him/her.*

Note: **Ayaw ko** is often shortened to **ayoko**.

Ayaw, gusto, kaya, kailangan + basic form

The doer is expressed as a Ng phrase (p. 70).

If the word preceding the basic form ends in a vowel or /n/, -ng may be added to it. See also: Na/-ng (p. 34)

Gustong kumain *ni Pedro*. **Gusto** *ni Pedro*ng ku**main**. **Gusto** *ni Pedro* ku**main**.	*Pedro wants to eat.*
Kayang magluto' *ni Pedro*. **Kaya** *ni Pedro*ng mag**luto'**. **Kaya** *ni Pedro* mag**luto'**.	*Pedro can cook.*

The doer is expressed as a Ng phrase, even when the basic form is a doer-POD verb.

Gustong kumain *ni Pedro* **ng mangga.** (doer-POD)	*Pedro wants to eat a mango / some mangoes.*
Gustong kainin *ni Pedro* **ang mangga.** (object-POD)	*Pedro wants to eat the mango.*
Gustong sulatan *ni Pedro* **ang teacher.** (direction-POD)	*Pedro wants to write the teacher.*

See also: Roles of the POD (p. 105)

Kailangan, dapat, pwede + verb/noun/etc.

If the word preceding the verb/noun/etc. ends in a vowel or /n/, -ng may be added to it. See also: Na/-ng (p. 34)

Kailangang kumain si Fred.	*Fred needs to eat.*
Dapat kumain si Fred.	*Fred should eat.*
Pwedeng kumain si Fred.	*Fred may eat.*

Kailangang estudyante si Fred.	*Fred needs to be a student.* *It's necessary for Fred to be a student.*
Dapat estudyante si Fred.	*Fred should be a student.* *Fred ought to be a student.*
Pwedeng estudyante si Fred.	*Fred could be a student.* *It's possible that Fred is a student.*

Dapat kumain si Fred ng mangga. (doer-POD)	*Fred should eat a mango / some mangoes.*
Dapat kainin ni Fred ang mangga. (object-POD)	*Fred should eat the mango.*

Repeated pseudo-verbs

Pseudo-verbs can be repeated to intensify their meaning. **Na/-ng** (p. 34) is placed after the first pseudo-verb.

<u>a</u>yaw *na* <u>a</u>yaw	*really don't like/want etc.*
gusto*ng* gusto	*really like, really want etc.*
<u>ka</u>ya*ng* <u>ka</u>ya	*really can etc.* (expressing ability)
<u>pwe</u>de*ng* <u>pwe</u>de	*really can etc.* (expressing possibility or permission)
kai<u>la</u>ngang kai<u>la</u>ngan	*really need etc.*
<u>da</u>pat *na* <u>da</u>pat (rarely used)	*really should etc.*

For the other meanings of the pseudo-verbs, see Pseudo-verbs: Overview (p. 236).

Sentences:

Gustong gusto ni John ang <u>ko</u>tse.	*John really likes/wants the car.*
Gustong gustong kum<u>a</u>in ni Pedro ng mangga.	*Pedro really wants to eat a mango / some mangoes.*

Adjectives

Identical adjectives and nouns

Some adjectives are identical to a noun except that the noun has a long vowel.

	adjective		noun
buhay	*alive*	**buhay**	*life*
galit	*angry*	**galit**	*anger*
gutom	*hungry*	**gutom**	*hunger*
pagod	*tired*	**pagod**	*tiredness*
sira'	*damaged*	**sira'**	*damage*
sunog	*burnt*	**sunog**	*fire*
tulog	*asleep*	**tulog**	*sleep*

See also: Long vowels (stress) (p. 21)

Gender

There are a few adjectives that have a form ending in /a/, which is used to describe female persons.

male	female	translation
<u>lo</u>ko	<u>lo</u>ka	*crazy*
ambi<u>syo</u>so	ambi<u>syo</u>sa	*ambitious*
ner<u>byo</u>so	ner<u>byo</u>sa	*nervous*

Affixed and unaffixed adjectives

Some adjectives don't have an affix while others do.

Examples of unaffixed adjectives:

gutom	*hungry*
busog	*full (having eaten enough)*
<u>pa</u>ngit	*ugly, undesirable*

Examples of adjectives made up of a root and an affix:

*ma*ganda	*pretty*
*ma*laki	*big*
*pala*away	*quarrelsome*

See also: Roots and affixes (p. 29)

Adjective affixes

The most common adjective affixes are given below, together with a number of examples.

The roots and root-affix combinations may have more meanings than the ones given here.

See also:

- Roots and affixes (p. 29)
- Sound changes when combining roots and affixes (p. 31)
- Syllable repetition (p. 33)

-in

prone to, susceptible to

root	meaning	root + affix	meaning
sakit	*illness*	sakitin	*prone to illness*
lagnat	*fever*	lagnatin	*prone to fevers*

sipon	*cold*	**sipunin**	*prone to colds*
antok	*sleepiness*	**antukin**	*prone to sleepiness*

Sentences:

Lagnatin si Ningning.	*Ningning is prone to fevers.*
Antukin si Gingging.	*Gingging is prone to sleepiness.*

ka-

having something in common

root	meaning	root + affix	meaning
pareho	*similar, same*	**kapareho**	*similar to, like*
tulad	*like*	**katulad**	*similar to, like*
mukha'	*face*	**kamukha'**	*identical to, looking like*
pantay	*equal, even, of equal height*	**kapantay**	*flush with, level with*
tumbas	*value*	**katumbas**	*of equal value to, equal to*
tabi	*side*	**katabi**	*beside, adjacent to*

Sentences:

Kamukha' ni Arnold si John.	*John looks like Arnold.*
Kapantay ng kabinet ang lamesa.	*The table is level with the cabinet.*

ka- +rep2

causing or producing something in an extreme degree

root	meaning	root + affix	meaning
galang	*respect*	kagalang-galang	*inspiring great respect*
paniwala'	*belief*	kapani-paniwala'	*very plausible*
tawa	*laughter*	katawa-tawa	*hilarious*
hiya'	*shame*	kahiya-hiya'	*very embarrassing*
takot	*fear*	katakot-takot	*terrible, terrifying, tremendous*

ma-

(the most common adjective affix)
having a certain quality or having a lot of something

root	meaning	root + affix	meaning
ganda	*beauty*	maganda	*beautiful*
laki	*size*	malaki	*big*
ulap	*cloud*	maulap	*cloudy*
alikabok	*dust*	maalikabok	*dusty*
bait	*kindness*	mabait	*kind*
tamis	*sweetness*	matamis	*sweet*
bilis	*speed*	mabilis	*fast*
bigat	*weight*	mabigat	*heavy*
init	*heat*	mainit	*hot*
talino	*intelligence*	matalino	*intelligent*
kulit	*importunity, irritating persistence*	makulit	*importunate, irritating, pesky, nagging*
hilig	*liking, inclination*	mahilig	*fond (of something)*

ma-...-in, ma- +rep1-...-in

having a certain quality to a high degree; or,
inclined to be

root	meaning	root + affix	meaning
<u>tu</u>long	*help*	matulungin	*helpful*
<u>a</u>wa'	*mercy, pity, compassion*	maawain	*merciful, compassionate*
<u>li</u>mot	*oblivion*	<u>ma</u>limutin malilimutin	*forgetful*
inggit	*envious*	main<u>gg</u>itin	*inclined to be envious*
inip	*bored, impatient*	ma<u>in</u>ipin	*inclined to be bored or impatient*
<u>ta</u>kot	*fear*	matakutin matatakutin	*easily frightened*

magka-

having something in common (describing two persons or things)

root	meaning	root + affix	meaning
pa<u>re</u>ho	*similar, same*	magkapa<u>re</u>ho	*similar to or like each other (for 2)*
<u>tu</u>lad	*like*	magka<u>tu</u>lad	*similar to or like each other (for 2)*

| mukha' | face | magkamukha' | identical to or looking like each other (for 2) |
| pantay | equal, even, of equal height | magkapantay | flush or level with each other (for 2) |

Sentences:

| Magkamukha' sina Arnold at John. | Arnold and John look alike. |
| Magkapantay ang kabinet at lamesa. | The cabinet and the table are level with each other. |

magkaka-

having something in common (describing three or more persons or things)

root	meaning	root + affix	meaning
pareho	similar, same	magkakapareho	similar to or like one another (for 3 or more)
tulad	like	magkakatulad	similar to or like one another (for 3 or more)

mukha'	face	magkaka-mukha'	identical to or looking like one another (for 3 or more)
pantay	equal, even, of equal height	magkakapantay	flush or level with one another (for 3 or more)

Sentences:

Magkakamukha' sina Arnold, Ed at John.	*Arnold, Ed and John look alike.*
Magkakapantay ang <u>ka</u>binet, <u>o</u>ven at la<u>me</u>sa.	*The cabinet, the oven and the table are level with one another.*

maka-
in favor of, pro-, fond of

root	meaning	root + affix	meaning
<u>ba</u>yan	*country, town*	maka<u>ba</u>yan	*patriotic*
<u>ba</u>go	*new*	maka<u>ba</u>go	*modern, progressive*
<u>lu</u>ma'	*old*	maka<u>lu</u>ma'	*old-fashioned*
Mandela	*Mandela*	maka-Mandela	*pro-Mandela*

mapag-

having a certain quality; having a habit of doing something; fond of doing something

root	meaning	root + affix	meaning
bigay	*giving*	**mapagbigay**	*generous*
mahal	*someone loved*	**mapagmahal**	*loving*
bi̲ro'	*joke*	**mapagbiro'**	*funny (someone who likes telling jokes)*
mu̲ra	*swearing, cuss word*	**mapagmura**	*(someone who) swears a lot*

naka-

in a certain position, state or condition; or,
wearing something

root	meaning	root + affix	meaning
harap	*front*	**nakaharap**	*facing*
higa'	*lying down*	**nakahiga'**	*lying down (in a lying position)*
tayo'	*standing*	**nakatayo'**	*standing (in a standing position)*

tira (seldom used on its own)	living (in/on/at)	nakatira	living (in/on/at)
upo'	sitting	nakaupo'	seated
salamin	glasses	nakasalamin	wearing glasses
sapatos	shoes	nakasapatos	wearing shoes
itim	black	nakaitim	wearing black
bukas	open	nakabukas	open, turned on

Sentences:

Nakasapatos si Raphael.	Raphael is wearing shoes.
Nakatira si Mimi sa Cebu.	Mimi lives in Cebu.

nakaka-
causing or producing something

root	meaning	root + affix	meaning
tawa	laughter	nakakatawa	funny
gulat	surprise	nakakagulat	startling
hiya'	shame, embarrassment	nakakahiya'	embarrassing
inis	annoyance, exasperation	nakakainis	annoying, exasperating

antok	*sleepiness*	na**ka**kaantok	*causing sleepiness*
takot	*fear*	na**ka**ka**ta**kot	*frightening, scary*
tuwa'	*joy, happiness*	na**ka**katuwa'	*funny, amusing, cute, pleasing*
sakit	*pain*	na**ka**kasakit	*causing pain, hurtful*

nakakapang-

causing or producing something

root	meaning	root + affix	meaning
hina'	*weakness*	na**ka**kapang-**hi**na'	*causing temporary weakness or depression*
hi**na**yang	*regret*	na**ka**kapang-hi**na**yang	*causing regret*

Sentences:

Na**ka**kapang**hi**na' ang ba**li**ta'.	*The news is depressing. The news is making me feel weak.*
Na**ka**kapanghi**na**yang ang nang**ya**ri.	*What happened is regrettable. The incident is regrettable.*

pa- [1]

in the manner of

root	meaning	root + affix	meaning
bulong	*whisper*	**pabulong**	*in a whisper*
dabog	*stamping of feet in irritation or anger*	**padabog**	*while stamping one's feet angrily*
tayo'	*standing*	**patayo'**	*vertical*
higa'	*lying down*	**pahiga'**	*horizontal*
tagilid	*tilted*	**patagilid**	*sideways*

Sentences:

Patayo' ang mga <u>lin</u>ya.	*The lines are vertical.*
Patagilid ang pag<u>kakaku</u>log ni Jun.	*Jun fell sideways.* Lit. *Jun's falling was sideways.*

pa- [2]

about to
often used with **na**

root	meaning	root + affix	meaning
dating	*arrival*	**parating**	*about to arrive*
alis	*departure*	**paalis**	*about to leave*

lubog	*sinking*	**palubog**	*about to sink or set*
uwi'	*going or coming home*	**pauwi'**	*about to go or come home*

Sentences:

Palubog na ang araw.	*The sun is about to set.*
Parating na si Mariel.	*Mariel is about to arrive.*

pa- +rep2

doing something now and then or here and there

root	meaning	root + affix	meaning
gala'	*wandering*	**pagala-gala'**	*wandering here and there*
sama	*joining, accompanying*	**pasama-sama**	*going along here and there*

Sentences:

Pagala-gala' sila.	*They are wandering here and there.*
Pasama-sama lang sila.	*They just tag along here and there.*

pala-

doing something a lot; fond of doing something

root	meaning	root + affix	meaning
b<u>i</u>ro'	*joke*	**palabiro'**	*funny (someone who likes telling jokes)*
ngiti'	*smile*	**palangiti'**	*smiley (someone who smiles a lot)*
<u>a</u>way	*quarrel*	**palaaway**	*quarrelsome*
<u>a</u>ral	*lesson, studying*	**palaaral**	*studious*
<u>ta</u>wa	*laughter*	**palatawa**	*(someone who) laughs a lot*
tanong	*question*	**palatanong**	*(someone who) asks a lot of questions*

pang-

for; intended for use or wear in/on/at

root	meaning	root + affix	meaning
<u>ba</u>hay	*house*	pam<u>ba</u>hay	*for wearing at home*
kasal	*wedding*	pangkasal	*for wearing at one's wedding (e.g. a wedding dress)*
dalawa	*two*	pandalawa	*for two*
<u>ba</u>ta'	*child (boy or girl)*	pam<u>ba</u>ta'	*for kids*

Sentences:

Pam<u>ba</u>hay ang T-shirt.	*The T-shirt is only worn at home.* Lit. *The T-shirt is for wearing at home.*
Pam<u>ba</u>ta' ang libro.	*The book is for kids.*

Compound adjectives

Some adjectives are made up of two words. Examples:

first word	second word	compound adjective
amoy *smell*	**isda'** *fish*	**amoy-isda'** *smelling of fish*
<u>la</u>sa *taste*	**isda'** *fish*	**<u>la</u>sang-isda'*** *tasting of fish*

* If the first word ends in a vowel or /**n**/, -**ng** is added to it. See also:
Na/-ng (p. 34)

Sentence:

Amoy-isda' si Pedro.	*Pedro smells of fish.*

Intensity

Intensifiers and downtoners

Group 1

intensifier / downtoner	meaning	example	meaning
... nang kaunti'	*a bit*	malaki nang kaunti'	*a bit big*
hindi' gaano -ng	*not very*	hindi' gaanong malaki	*not very big*
hindi' masyado -ng	*not so, not that*	hindi' masyadong malaki	*not so big*
medyo	*pretty, rather, quite*	medyo malaki	*pretty big, rather big*
talaga (-ng)	*really*	talagang malaki, malaki talaga	*really big*
masyado (-ng)	*too*	masyadong malaki, malaki masyado	*too big*

See also: **Na/-ng** (p. 34)

Group 2 (followed by the root)

Group 2 intensifiers are combined with the root.

intensifier	meaning	example	meaning
ang	*how, so*	**ang laki!**	*how big!*
ang rep2	*how (very), so*	**ang laki-laki!**	*how (very) big!*
		ang ta<u>li</u>-ta<u>li</u>no	*how (very) smart*
<u>na</u>**paka-**	*how, so*	<u>na</u>**pakalaki**	*so big*
<u>so</u>**bra -ng**	*how, so*	<u>so</u>**bra*n*g laki**	*so big*
pa<u>gka</u>- +rep2	*how extremely*	**pa<u>gka</u>laki-laki!**	*how extremely big!*
		pa<u>gka</u>ta<u>li</u>-ta<u>li</u>no	*how extremely smart*

See also: **Na/-ng** (p. 34), Syllable repetition (p. 33)

When a Group 2 intensifier is used, the person or thing described is expressed as a Ng phrase (p. 70).

<u>Me</u>dyo malaki *ang* *<u>a</u>so*.	*The dog is pretty big.*
<u>Na</u>pakalaki *ng* *<u>a</u>so*.	*The dog is so big.*

<u>Me</u>dyo malaki *iyan*.	*That's pretty big.*
<u>Na</u>pakalaki *niyan*.	*That's so big.*

Repeated adjectives

An adjective can be repeated to intensify its meaning. **Na/-ng** (p. 34) is placed after the first adjective. Examples:

maliit	*small*	maliit *na* maliit	*very small*
malaki	*big*	malaki*ng* malaki	*very big*
pagod	*tired*	pagod *na* pagod	*very tired*

Repeated non-adjective roots

A few non-adjective roots can also be repeated, turning them into intensified adjectives. Examples:

awa'	*pity*	awa*ng* awa'	*feeling great pity*
tuwa'	*joy, happiness*	tuwa*ng* tuwa'	*very happy*

Adjectives with syllable repetition

For **ma-** adjectives:
ma- +rep2 – *pretty, quite, rather...*

maliit	*small*	maliit-liit	*pretty small*
ma<u>la</u>pit	*near*	malapit-lapit	*quite near*
masarap	*tasty*	masarap-sarap	*quite tasty*

For some unaffixed adjectives:
rep2 – *thoroughly, completely, full of, all...*

sira'	*broken, damaged*	si<u>ra</u>-sira'	*completely broken or worn out*
hiwalay	*separated*	hi<u>wa</u>-hiwalay	*thoroughly separated or scattered*
butas	*having a hole*	butas-butas	*full of holes*
baliktad	*upside down, inside out, back to front*	ba<u>li</u>-baliktad	*all topsy-turvy, jumbled or mixed up*

See also:

- **Ma-** adjectives (p. 246)
- Affixed and unaffixed adjectives (p. 242)
- Syllable repetition (p. 33)

Plural adjectives

The following adjectives can be made plural:

1. **Ma-** adjectives
Plural: **ma-** +rep1

singular	plural	meaning
maliit	ma*li*liit	*small*
malaki	ma*la*laki	*big*

2. Adjective roots and some unaffixed adjectives intensified by a Group 2 intensifier
Plural: **ang/<u>na</u>paka-/<u>so</u>brang** +rep1

singular	plural	meaning
ang liit	ang *li*liit	*so small*
<u>na</u>pakaliit	<u>na</u>paka*li*liit	*so small*
<u>so</u>brang liit	<u>so</u>brang *li*liit	*so small*
ang <u>mu</u>ra	ang *mu*<u>mu</u>ra	*so cheap*
<u>na</u>paka<u>mu</u>ra	<u>na</u>paka*mu*<u>mu</u>ra	*so cheap*
<u>so</u>brang <u>mu</u>ra	<u>so</u>brang *mu*<u>mu</u>ra	*so cheap*

Note: Using the plural forms is optional.

Ang <u>mu</u>ra ng mga T-shirt. **Ang *mu*<u>mu</u>ra ng mga T-shirt.**	*The T-shirts are so cheap.*

See also:

- **Ma-** adjectives (p. 246)
- Affixed and unaffixed adjectives (p. 242)
- Syllable repetition (p. 33)
- Group 2 intensifiers (p. 259)
- Noun plurals (p. 78)

Comparing persons or things

Equality

sing- / kasing-

as... as

used when comparing with one person or thing

*sing*ganda *kasing*ganda	*as pretty as*
*sim*bilis *kasim*bilis	*as fast as*
*sin*tangkad *kasin*tangkad	*as tall as*

Sentence:

Kasintangkad ni John si Paul.	*Paul is as tall as John.*

See also: Sound changes when combining roots and affixes (p. 31)

sing- +rep1 / kasing- +rep1

as... as

used when comparing with two or more persons or things

*singga*ganda *kasingga*ganda	*as pretty as (2 or more)*
*simbi*bilis *kasimbi*bilis	*as fast as (2 or more)*
*sinta*tangkad *kasinta*tangkad	*as tall as (2 or more)*

Sentence:

Kasintatangkad nina John at Mark si Paul.	*Paul is as tall as John and Mark.*

See also: Sound changes when combining roots and affixes (p. 31), Syllable repetition (p. 33)

magsing- / magkasing-

equally, as... as each other

describing two persons or things

*magsing*ganda *magkasing*ganda	*equally pretty (for 2),* *as pretty as each other*
*magsim*bilis *magkasim*bilis	*equally fast (for 2),* *as fast as each other*
*magsin*tangkad *magkasin*tangkad	*equally tall (for 2),* *as tall as each other*

Sentence:

Magkasintangkad sina John at Paul.	*John and Paul are as tall as each other.*

See also: Sound changes when combining roots and affixes (p. 31)

magsising- / magkakasing-

equally, as... as one another
describing three or more persons or things

*magsising*ganda *magkakasing*ganda	*equally pretty (for 3 or more), as pretty as one another*
*magsisim*bilis *magkakasim*bilis	*equally fast (for 3 or more), as fast as one another*
*magsisin*tangkad *magkakasin*tangkad	*equally tall (for 3 or more), as tall as one another*

Sentence:

Magkakasintangkad sina John, Mark at Paul.	*John, Mark and Paul are as tall as one another.*

See also: Sound changes when combining roots and affixes (p. 31)

Inequality

hindi' kasing-

not as... as

Hindi' kasintangkad ni John si **Paul.**	*Paul is not as tall as John.*

See also: Sound changes when combining roots and affixes (p. 31)

mas... (kaysa) + Sa phrase

more.../-er than

Mas matangkad si John *kaysa sa* <u>ba</u>**ta'.** **Mas** matangkad si John *sa* <u>ba</u>**ta'.**	*John is taller than the child.*
Mas matangkad si John *kaysa kay* **Paul.** **Mas** matangkad si John *kay* **Paul.**	*John is taller than Paul.*

See also: Sa phrase (p. 70)

Superlative

pinaka-

most.../-est

Pinaka- is affixed to the whole adjective, and not just to the root.

*pinaka*maganda	*prettiest*
*pinaka*mabilis	*fastest*
*pinaka*matangkad	*tallest*

Sentences:

Pinakamatangkad si John.	*John is the tallest.*
Si John ang pinakamatangkad.	*The tallest is John.*
Si John ang pinakamatangkad sa kanilang lahat.	*John is the tallest of them all.*

Other describing words

Expressing quantity or distribution

Cardinal numbers

1	isa	11	labing-isa	10	sampu'
2	dalawa	12	labindalawa	20	dalawampu'
3	tatlo	13	labintatlo	30	tatlumpu'
4	apat	14	labing-apat	40	apatnapu'
5	lima	15	labinlima	50	limampu'
6	anim	16	labing-anim	60	animnapu'
7	pito	17	labimpito	70	pitumpu'
8	walo	18	labingwalo	80	walumpu'
9	siyam	19	labinsiyam	90	siyamnapu'

100	isang daan	1,000	isang libo
	sandaan		sanlibo
200	dalawang daan	2,000	dalawang libo
300	tatlong daan	3,000	tatlong libo
400	apat na raan	4,000	apat na libo
500	limang daan	5,000	limang libo
600	anim na raan	6,000	anim na libo
700	pitong daan	7,000	pitong libo
800	walong daan	8,000	walong libo
900	siyam na raan	9,000	siyam na libo

10,000	sampung libo
1,000,000	isang milyon
21	dalawampu't isa
85	walumpu't lima
371	tatlong daan, pitumpu't isa

Note: 't is short for **at** (*"and"*).

Sentences:

Dalawa ang <u>ko</u>tse.	*There are two cars.* Lit. *The cars are two.*
Dalawa ang anak ni John.	*John has two children.* Lit. *The children of John are two.*

Note: **Mga** cannot be placed before <u>ko</u>tse or **anak**. If the News (p. 35) of the sentence is a number, **mga** cannot be used in the POD (p. 35). See also: Noun plurals (p. 78)

Phrases:

dalawa*n*g ba<u>ba</u>e	*two women*
dalawa sa mga ba<u>ba</u>e	*two of the women*
dalawa sa kanila	*two of them*
sila*n*g dalawa	*the two of them*
dalawa nito	*two of these*

See also: **Na/-ng** (p. 34), Sa phrase (p. 70), Ng phrase (p. 70)

Spanish-derived cardinal numbers

1	uno	11	onse	10	dyes
2	dos	12	dose	20	bente
3	tres	13	trese	30	trenta
4	kwatro	14	katorse	40	kwarenta
5	singko	15	kinse	50	singkwenta
6	sais	16	dyesisais	60	sisenta
7	syete	17	dyesisyete	70	sitenta
8	otso	18	dyesiotso	80	otsenta
9	nwebe	19	dyesinwebe	90	nobenta

1,000	mil
21	bente uno
31	trenta'y uno
57	singkwenta'y syete

Ordinal numbers

	informal	formal
1st	<u>u</u>na	<u>u</u>na
2nd	pangalawa	ikalawa
3rd	pangatlo	ikatlo
4th	pang-<u>a</u>pat	ika<u>a</u>pat
5th	panlima	ikalima
6th	pang-<u>a</u>nim	ika<u>a</u>nim
7th	pampito	ikapito
8th	pangwalo	ikawalo
9th	pansiyam	ikasiyam
10th	pansampu'	ikasampu'
11th	panlabing-isa	ikalabing-isa
51st	panlimampu't isa	ikalimampu't isa
100th	pansandaan	ikasandaan

Fractions

The only commonly-used fraction expression is **kala<u>h</u>ati'** (½). Other
fractions are usually expressed in English (e.g. *one-fourth, one-third*).

Other number expressions

In twos etc.

rep2	-an	meaning
isa-isa	isahan	in ones, one by one, one at a time
dala-dalawa	dalawahan	in twos, in pairs, two at a time
tatlu-tatlo	tatluhan	in threes, three at a time
apat-apat	apatan	in fours, four at a time
lima-lima	limahan	in fives, five at a time
sampu-sampu'	sampuan	in tens, ten at a time
dala-dalawampu'	dalawampuan	in groups of 20, 20 at a time

Rep2 can also express the idea of excessive number.

Dala-dalawa ang laptop niya.	He/she has two laptops. Lit. His/her laptops are two. (when only one is needed or expected)

See also: Syllable repetition (p. 33), Cardinal numbers (p. 269)

Only two etc.

rep1	meaning
iisa	*only 1*
dadalawa	*only 2*
tatatlo	*only 3*
aapat	*only 4*
lilima	*only 5*
sasampu'	*only 10*
dadalawampu'	*only 20*

See also: Syllable repetition (p. 33)

Only in twos etc.

rep1 +rep2	meaning
iisa-isa	*only in ones*
dadala-dalawa	*only in twos*
tatatlu-tatlo	*only in threes*
aapat-apat	*only in fours*
lilima-lima	*only in fives*

<u>sa</u>sam<u>pu</u>-sampu'	*only in tens*
<u>da</u>da<u>la</u>-dalawampu'	*only in groups of 20*

See also: Syllable repetition (p. 33)

Two each (for two persons or things) etc.

tig-	meaning
tig-isa	*1 each (for two persons or things)*
tigdalawa tigalawa	*2 each (for two persons or things)*
tigtatlo tigatlo	*3 each (for two persons or things)*
tig-<u>a</u>pat	*4 each (for two persons or things)*
tiglima	*5 each (for two persons or things)*
tigsampu'	*10 each (for two persons or things)*
tigdalawampu'	*20 each (for two persons or things)*

Two each (for three or more persons or things) etc.

tig- +rep1	tig- +rep2	meaning
tig-iisa	tig-isa-isa tigi-tigisa	1 each (for 3 or more persons or things)
tigdadalawa	tigdala-dalawa tiga-tigalawa	2 each (for 3 or more persons or things)
tigtatatlo	tigtatlu-tatlo tiga-tigatlo	3 each (for 3 or more persons or things)
tig-aapat	tig-apat-apat	4 each (for 3 or more persons or things)
tiglilima	tiglima-lima	5 each (for 3 or more persons or things)
tigsasampu'	tigsampu-sampu'	10 each (for 3 or more persons or things)
tigdadalawampu'	tigdala-dalawampu'	20 each (for 3 or more persons or things)

See also: Syllable repetition (p. 33)

Hundreds etc.

daan-daan	*hundreds*
l<u>i</u>bu-l<u>i</u>bo	*thousands*
milyun-milyon	*millions*

Numbers in use

Tagalog, English and Spanish-derived numbers are often used interchangeably. The tables below show the preferred language(s) in everyday conversation.

Dates	October 3 (three) 1970 (nineteen seventy)
Time	limang mi<u>nu</u>to, five minutes limang <u>o</u>ras, five hours
Clock time	three o'clock, alas tres

Age	tatlong taon, three years old
Percentage	sampung por<u>sye</u>nto, ten percent

Money	1 – piso 2 – dalawang piso, two pesos 10 – sampung piso, ten pesos 20 – dalawampung piso, twenty pesos, bente pesos 50 – limampung piso, fifty pesos, singkwenta pesos 75 – seventy-five pesos 100 – sandaang piso, one hundred pesos
Length	limang metro, five meters limang kilometro, five kilometers
Volume	limang kutsarita, five teaspoons limang kutsara, five tablespoons limang tasa, five cups limang litro, five liters limang galon, five gallons
Weight	limang kilo, five kilos five pounds
Addresses	5 (five) Ipil Street 1100 (one one zero zero)
Grade levels	grade one fourth year
Other	limang pares (5 pairs) limang dosena (5 dozens)

See also: Cardinal numbers (p. 269), Clock time (p. 302)

Other words expressing quantity or distribution

ilan

a few, some

ilang ba**bae**	*a few/some women*
ilan sa mga ba**bae**	*a few/some of the women*
ilan sa kanila	*a few/some of them*
ilan sa mga ito	*a few/some of these*

iilan

very few

iilang ba**bae**	*very few women*
iilan sa mga ba**bae**	*very few of the women*
iilan sa kanila	*very few of them*
iilan sa mga ito	*very few of these*

ma**ra**mi

a lot, much, many

ma**ra**ming ba**bae**	*many women*
ma**ra**mi sa mga ba**bae**	*many of the women*
ma**ra**mi sa kanila	*many of them*

marami sa mga ito	many of these
marami nito	a lot of this also: there are many of these*

* See also: **May, mayroon/meron, marami, wala'** (p. 379)

kaunti'
a little

kaunting asukal	a little sugar
kaunti' nito	a little of this

kakaunti'
very little

kakaunting asukal	very little sugar
kakaunti' nito	very little of this

kalahati'
half

kalahating kilo	half a kilo
kalahati' ng cake	half of the cake
kalahati' nito	half of this

kapiraso
a piece

kapirasong tela	*a piece of cloth*
kapiraso ng tela	*a piece of the cloth*
kapiraso nito	*a piece of this*

parte
part

parte ng grupo	*part of the group*
parte nito	*part of this*

karamihan
most

karamihan sa/ng mga babae	*most (of the) women*
karamihan sa kanila	*most of them*
karamihan sa/ng mga ito	*most of these*

lahat
all, everything, everyone

lahat ng babae	*all women*
lahat ng mga babae	*all the women*

lahat sila	*they all*
sila*ng* lahat	*all of them*
lahat ng ito	*all of this*
lahat ng mga ito	*all of these*
lahat ito	*all this*

<u>ba</u>wa't

each, every

<u>ba</u>wa't ba<u>ba</u>e	*every woman*
<u>ba</u>wa't isa sa mga ba<u>ba</u>e	*each of the women*
<u>ba</u>wa't isa sa kanila	*each of them*
<u>ba</u>wa't isa sa mga ito	*each of these*

Expressing similarity

Gaya, ganito, ganito ka-

g<u>a</u>ya/kag<u>a</u>ya + Ng phrase
like...

<u>Ga</u>ya ni Fred si John.	_John is like Fred._
<u>Ga</u>ya ng p<u>u</u>sa' ko ang p<u>u</u>sa' mo.	_Your cat is like my cat._

See also: Ng phrase (p. 70)

ganito, ganyan, ganoon

ganito	_like this (near me)_
ganyan	_like that (near you)_
ganoon	_like that (far from you and me)_

Sentences:

Ganyan si Fred.	_Fred is like that._
Ganito ang bag ko.	_My bag is like this._

Note: **Ganyan** can also be spelled as **ganiyan**.

See also: Clarification: near me etc. (p. 56)

ganito/ganyan/ganoon ka-

this/that...

ganito kalaki	*this big* *as big as this*
ganito katangkad	*this tall* *as tall as this*

Sentences:

Ganito katangkad si Fred.	*Fred is this tall.*
Ganyan katangkad si Fred.	*Fred is that tall.* *Fred is as tall as that (near* *you).*
Ganoon katangkad si Fred.	*Fred is that tall.* *Fred is as tall as that (far from* *you and me).*

The expressions can be made plural by means of rep1.

Ganito katangkad sina Fred at John. **Ganito kata̱tangkad sina Fred at John.**	*Fred and John are this tall.*

Note: Using the plural form is optional.

See also: Syllable repetition (p. 33)

Para

para -ng

like...

Parang si Fred si John.	*John is like Fred.*
Parang ang **pu**sa' ko ang **pu**sa' mo.	*Your cat is like my cat.*
Parang si Fred siya. **Para** siya*ng* si Fred.	*He's like Fred.*
Parang **ba**ta' siya. **Para** siya*ng* **ba**ta'.	*He/she's like a child.*

Note: **Para -ng** can also mean *it seems* or *seems (to be/like/that)*.

Parang masaya si John.	*John seems (to be) happy.*

See also: **Na/-ng** (p. 34), Enclitic words (p. 339)

Tulad

tulad/katulad + Ng phrase

like...

Tulad ni Fred si John.	*John is like Fred.*
Tulad ng pusa' ko ang pusa' mo.	*Your cat is like my cat.*

See also: Ng phrase (p. 70)

Mukha'

mukha' -ng

looks like (a/an)

Mukhang artista si John.	*John looks like an actor.*

Note: **Mukha' -ng** can also mean *it seems, seems (to be/like/that)* or *looks*.

Mukhang masarap ang cake.	*The cake looks delicious.*

See also: **Na/-ng** (p. 34)

kamukha' + Ng phrase

looks like (a particular person or thing)

Kamukha' ni Arnold si John.	*John looks like Arnold.*

See also: Ng phrase (p. 70)

Expressing manner

Describing words expressing manner are used as follows:

1. When used at the beginning of a sentence, they are often followed by **na/-ng**. Examples:

Mabilis na **tumakbo si John.**	*John ran fast.*
Patagilid na **nahulog si John.**	*John fell sideways.*
Parang luku-lukong **sumigaw si John.**	*John screamed like a madman.*

2. When used elsewhere in a sentence, they are preceded by **nang** or, in a few cases, by **na/-ng**.

Tumakbo si John *nang mabilis.*	*John ran fast.*
Nahulog si John *nang patagilid.*	*John fell sideways.*
Sumigaw si John *na parang luku-luko.*	*John screamed like a madman.*

Other examples of describing words expressing manner:

biglang	*nang* bigla'	*suddenly*
da<u>la</u>-dalawang	*nang* da<u>la</u>-dalawa	*in twos*
<u>ga</u>ya ng <u>ko</u>tse*(ng)*	*nang* <u>ga</u>ya ng <u>ko</u>tse	*like a car*
ganito kabilis *(na)*	*nang* ganito kabilis	*this fast*
um<u>ii</u>yak *na*	*na* um<u>ii</u>yak	*crying*

See also: **Na/-ng** (p. 34)

Expressing location

Na<u>s</u>a

Na<u>s</u>a indicates where someone or something is. It is equivalent to *(is/are/was/were) in/on/at etc.*

<u>na</u>sa May<u>ni</u>la'	*(is) in Manila*
<u>na</u>sa <u>ba</u>hay	*(is) at home*
<u>na</u>sa <u>me</u>sa	*(is) on the table*
<u>na</u>sa <u>a</u>kin	*(is) with me* *(is) in my possession*
<u>na</u>sa <u>a</u>min	*(is) with us* *(is) in our possession* *(is) at our place*

na kay Fred	(is) with Fred
	(is) in Fred's possession
na kina Fred	(is) with Fred and company
	(is) in Fred and company's possession
	(is) at Fred's place

Sentences:

Nasa Maynila' si John.	John is in Manila.
Nasa amin si John.	John is at our place.
Na kay Fred ang susi'.	Fred has the key.
	Lit. The key is with Fred.

Note: Both **nasa** and **sa** may be used to indicate where a place is. **Sa** may also be used to indicate where something happens.

Nasa Maynila' ang hotel.	The hotel is in Manila.
Sa Maynila' ang hotel.	
Sa Maynila' ang party.	The party is in Manila.

See also: **Sa** (p. 292), **Wala' sa, wala' rito** (p. 294)

Nan<u>di</u>to, nandiyan, nandoon

singular or plural	plural	meaning
nan<u>di</u>to <u>na</u>rito	nandi<u>di</u>to <u>na</u>ririto	*(is/are/was/were) here (near me)*
nandiyan <u>na</u>riyan	nandidiyan <u>na</u>ririyan	*(is/are/was/were) there (near you)*
nandoon <u>na</u>roon	nandodoon <u>na</u>roroon	*(is/are/was/were) over there (far from you and me)*

Note:

1. Using the plural forms is optional.

2. **Nandoon** and **<u>na</u>roon** may be shortened to **nandon / nandun / andon / andun** and **<u>na</u>ron**, respectively, in spoken Tagalog.

Sentences:

Nan<u>di</u>to si John.	*John is here.*
Nan<u>di</u>to sina John at Paul. **Nandi<u>di</u>to sina John at Paul.**	*John and Paul are here.*

See also: Clarification: near me etc. (p. 56), **Wala' sa, wala' <u>ri</u>to** (p. 294)

Sa

sa May<u>ni</u>la'	*in Manila, to Manila etc.*
sa <u>ba</u>hay	*at home, to the house etc.*
sa <u>me</u>sa	*on the table, to the table etc.*
sa <u>a</u>kin	*to me, through me etc.*
sa <u>a</u>min	*to us, at our place etc.*
kay Fred	*to Fred, through Fred etc.*
kina Fred	*to Fred and company, at Fred's place etc.*

Sentences:

Pumunta sa May<u>ni</u>la' si John.	*John went to Manila.*
Ku<u>ma</u>in sa <u>a</u>min si John.	*John ate at our place.*
Na<u>tu</u>log kina Fred si John.	*John slept at Fred's place.*

See also:

- Sa markers: indicating location or direction (p. 50)
- <u>Na</u>sa (p. 289)

<u>Di</u>to, diyan, doon

<u>di</u>to, <u>ri</u>to	*here (near me)*
diyan, riyan	*there (near you)*
doon, roon	*over there (far from you and me)*

Sentences:

Ku<u>ma</u>in doon si John.	*John ate there.*
Pumunta doon si John.	*John went there.*

See also: Clarification: near me etc. (p. 56)

<u>E</u>to, ayan, ayun

<u>E</u>to, ayan and **ayun** are used to introduce or point to someone or something.

<u>e</u>to **he**to	*here is/are (near me)*
ayan **hayan**	*there is/are (near you)*
ayun **hayun**	*there is/are (far from you and me)*

Sentences:

<u>E</u>to ang <u>su</u>lat.	*Here's the letter.*
<u>E</u>to.	*Here it is.*

See also: Clarification: near me etc. (p. 56)

Wala' sa, wala' rito

The opposite of **nasa** is **wala' sa**.

Wala' sa – *(is/are/was/were) not in/on/at etc.*

Wala' sa Maynila' si John.	John isn't in Manila.
Wala' sa amin si John.	John isn't at our place.
Wala' kay Fred ang susi'.	Fred doesn't have the key. Lit. The key isn't with Fred.

The opposite of **nandito** is **wala' dito** or **wala' rito**.

Wala' rito si John.	John isn't here.
Wala' roon si John.	John isn't there.

Wala' can also stand alone and mean *(is/are/was/were) not here/there*.

Wala' si John.	John isn't here/there.

See also:

- Nasa (p. 289)
- Nandito, nandiyan, nandoon (p. 291)
- May, mayroon/meron, marami, wala' (p. 379)

May

Nasa and sa can be followed by **may** to indicate approximate location.

Nasa post office si John.	*John is (standing) at the post office.*
Nasa *may* post office si John.	*John is (standing) near the post office.*

Naghihintay *sa* post office si John.	*John is waiting at the post office.*
Naghihintay *sa may* post office si John.	*John is waiting near the post office.*

See also: Nasa (p. 289), **Sa** (p. 292)

Positions

loob	interior, inside	sa/nasa loob ng	inside
labas	exterior, outside	sa/nasa labas ng	outside
harap harapan	front	sa/nasa harap ng sa/nasa harapan ng	in front of
tapat	front (place facing the front of)	sa/nasa tapat ng	in front of, facing the front of
likod likuran	back	sa/nasa likod ng sa/nasa likuran ng	behind
tabi gilid	side	sa/nasa tabi ng sa/nasa gilid ng	beside
kanan	right	sa/nasa kanan ng	on/to the right of
kaliwa'	left	sa/nasa kaliwa' ng	on/to the left of
kabila'	other side	sa/nasa kabila' ng	on the other side of
ibabaw	place above	sa/nasa ibabaw ng	on top of
ilalim	place beneath	sa/nasa ilalim ng	below, under

itaas taas	*upper part,* *upstairs,* *higher up*	sa/<u>na</u>sa itaas ng sa/<u>na</u>sa taas ng	*in the upper* *part of, at the* *top of*
ibaba' baba'	*lower part,* *downstairs,* *lower down*	sa/<u>na</u>sa ibaba' ng sa/<u>na</u>sa baba' ng	*in the lower* *part of, at the* *bottom of*

gitna'	*middle*	sa/<u>na</u>sa gitna' ng	*in the middle* *of*
<u>pagi</u>tan	*space between*	sa/<u>na</u>sa pag<u>i</u>tan ng	*between*
<u>dul</u>o	*end*	sa/<u>na</u>sa <u>dul</u>o ng	*at the end of*
<u>kan</u>to	*(street) corner*	sa/<u>na</u>sa <u>kan</u>to ng	*at the corner* *of*

Sentences:

<u>Na</u>sa i<u>la</u>lim ng <u>ka</u>ma ang <u>pu</u>sa'.	*The cat is under the bed.*
Na<u>tutu</u>log sa i<u>la</u>lim ng <u>ka</u>ma ang <u>pu</u>sa'.	*The cat is sleeping under the bed.*

See also: <u>Na</u>sa (p. 289), Sa (p. 292), Ng phrase (p. 70)

Expressing source or destination

mula' (sa)

from

mula' (sa) Maynila'	*from Manila*
mula' roon	*from there*
Naglakad siya mula' Quezon City.	*He/she walked from Quezon City.*

hanggang (sa)

to

hanggang (sa) Maynila'	*to Manila*
mula' rito hanggang doon	*from here to there*
Naglakad siya mula' Quezon City hanggang Alabang.	*He/she walked from Quezon City to Alabang.*

galing (sa)

from, coming from

galing (sa) Maynila'	*(coming) from Manila*
galing doon	*(coming) from there*
Galing sa Belgium ang mga tsokolate.	*The chocolates are from Belgium.*

papunta sa

going to, bound for

papunta sa May<u>ni</u>la'	*going to Manila*
papunta roon	*going there*
Papunta sa May<u>ni</u>la' ang bus.	*The bus is going to Manila.*

Expressing extent

Nang may be used to show the extent of a difference or change in amount, quantity, size, degree etc. (*"by"*).

tumaas nang 10%	*increased by 10%*
bumigat nang 5 <u>ki</u>lo	*got heavier by 5 kilos*
bumigat nang kaunti'	*got a bit heavy*
mas ma<u>ha</u>ba' nang 5 <u>me</u>tro	*longer by 5 meters*
mas ma<u>ha</u>ba' nang kaunti'	*a bit longer*

Expressing time, frequency or duration

Month names

E**ne**ro	*January*
Peb**re**ro	*February*
Marso	*March*
Abril	*April*
Mayo	*May*
Hunyo	*June*
Hulyo	*July*
A**gos**to	*August*
Set**yem**bre	*September*
Ok**tu**bre	*October*
Nob**yem**bre	*November*
Dis**yem**bre	*December*

Note: English month names are also often used in Tagalog.

Days of the week

Linggo	*Sunday*
Lunes	*Monday*
Martes	*Tuesday*
Miyerkules	*Wednesday*
Huwebes	*Thursday*
Biyernes	*Friday*
Sabado	*Saturday*

Note: English day names are also often used in Tagalog.

Parts of the day

umaga	*morning*
tanghali'	*noon*
hapon	*afternoon*
gabi	*evening, night*
hatinggabi	*midnight*
madaling-araw	*wee hours*

Clock time

1:00 am	ala una	ng madaling-araw
2:00 am	alas dos	ng umaga
3:00 am	alas tres	
4:00 am	alas kwatro	
5:00 am	alas singko	
6:00 am	alas sais	ng umaga
7:00 am	alas syete	
8:00 am	alas otso	
9:00 am	alas nwebe	
10:00 am	alas dyes	
11:00 am	alas onse	
12:00 noon	alas dose	ng tanghali'
1:00 pm	ala una	ng hapon
2:00 pm	alas dos	
3:00 pm	alas tres	
4:00 pm	alas kwatro	
5:00 pm	alas singko	

6:00 pm	alas sais	ng gabi
7:00 pm	alas syete	
8:00 pm	alas otso	
9:00 pm	alas nwebe	
10:00 pm	alas dyes	
11:00 pm	alas onse	
12:00 midnight	alas dose	ng gabi ng hatinggabi

3:30	alas tres y medya*
7:30	alas syete y medya

* **Y** is pronounced as *"i."*

It is also common to tell the time in English by saying the numbers in groups of two (e.g. **seven thirty**). Expressions such as **quarter to...**, **twenty to...**, **ten to...** and **... quarter** (for *quarter past...*) are also often used.

Note:

alas kwatro	*four o'clock* *at four o'clock*
Alas kwatro na.	*It's four o'clock.*

See also: Parts of the Day (p. 301)

General time expressions

noon	*then, at that time (in the past)*
kamakalawa	*the day before yesterday*
ka<u>ha</u>pon	*yesterday*
kagabi	*last night*
ngayon	*today, now*
<u>bu</u>kas	*tomorrow*

ki<u>na</u>uma<u>ga</u>han	*the following morning*
ki<u>na</u>bu<u>ka</u>san	*the following day* also: *future*
ki<u>na</u>gabihan	*the following night*

ka<u>ni</u>na	*earlier today*
ngayon-ngayon lang	*just now*
ka<u>ni</u>-ka<u>ni</u>na lang	*just a while ago*
ka<u>ha</u>-ka<u>ha</u>pon lang	*just yesterday*

<u>ma</u>maya'	*later today*
ma<u>ya</u>-maya'	*in a little while (soon)*
agad, kaagad	*right away*

(nang) buong u<u>ma</u>ga*	*all morning*
(nang) buong linggo*	*all week*
(nang) buong taon*	*all year*
(nang) (buong) mag<u>ha</u>pon*	*all day*
(nang) (buong) magdamag*	*all night*

(nang) madalas*	*often*
bi<u>hi</u>ra'	*seldom*
<u>min</u>san	*sometimes, once (one time)*
<u>min</u>san-<u>min</u>san, pa<u>min</u>san-<u>min</u>san	*sometimes, occasionally*
<u>la</u>gi, pa<u>la</u>gi, pa<u>ra</u>ti	*always*

| (nang) sandali'* | *a while, a moment, for a minute* |

<u>o</u>ras-<u>o</u>ras	*every hour*
<u>a</u>raw-<u>a</u>raw	*every day*
gabi-gabi	*every night*
linggo-linggo	*every week*
buwan-buwan	*every month*
taon-taon	*every year*

* **Nang** is dropped when the time expression is used at the beginning of a sentence.

Time expressions with an introducing word

sa

indicates future time

sa **Lu**nes	*next Monday, this Monday*
sa E**ne**ro	*next January*
sa isang linggo	*next week, in one week (from now)*
sa **su**sunod na linggo	*next week*
sa mga **su**sunod na linggo	*in the coming weeks*
sa loob ng tatlong linggo	*within three weeks, in three weeks*
sa makalawa	*the day after tomorrow*
sa katapusan ng buwan	*at the end of the month*

noong

indicates past time
often shortened to **nung**

noong **Lu**nes	*last Monday*
noong E**ne**ro	*last January*
noong isang linggo	*last week*
noong nakaraang linggo	*a week ago*
noong mga nakaraang linggo	*during the past weeks*

| noong 1977 | *in 1977* |
| noong panahon ng WWII | *during/at the time of WWII* |

nang

introduces a time expression without specifying whether it is in the past or in the future. It is dropped when the time expression is used at the beginning of a sentence.

nang Lunes	*on a Monday*
nang Enero	*in January (one January)*
nang ala una	*at one o'clock*
nang mga ala una	*at around one o'clock*
nang pasado ala una	*after one o'clock*
nang umaga	*in the morning (one morning)*

Nang can also be used to indicate frequency or duration.

| kumain nang tatlong beses sa isang araw | *eat three times a day* Lit. *eat three times in one day* |
| naghintay nang tatlong oras | *waited for three hours* |

kung, kapag, pag

when

kung u<u>ma</u>ga pag u<u>ma</u>ga	*mornings*
kung <u>Lu</u>nes pag <u>Lu</u>nes	*on Mondays*
kung E<u>ne</u>ro pag E<u>ne</u>ro	*when it's January (in January)*
kung <u>min</u>san	*sometimes*

tuwing

every

tuwing u<u>ma</u>ga	*every morning*
tuwing <u>Lu</u>nes	*every Monday*
tuwing E<u>ne</u>ro	*every January*
tuwing Pasko	*every Christmas*

<u>ka</u>da

every

<u>ka</u>da <u>o</u>ras	*every hour*
<u>ka</u>da <u>a</u>raw	*every day*
<u>ka</u>da buwan	*every month*
<u>ka</u>da taon	*every year*

mula'

since, starting, from... (onwards)

mula' sa <u>Lu</u>nes	*from Monday (onwards)*
mula' noong <u>Lu</u>nes	*since last Monday*
mula' noong E<u>ne</u>ro	*since last January*
mula' ala <u>u</u>na	*from one o'clock (onwards)*
mula' noon	*since then*
mula' ka<u>ha</u>pon	*since yesterday*
mula' ngayon	*from now on, starting today*
mula' <u>bu</u>kas	*starting tomorrow*

hanggang

until, up to

hanggang sa <u>Lu</u>nes	*until next Monday, until this Monday*
hanggang noong <u>Lu</u>nes	*until last Monday*
hanggang noong E<u>ne</u>ro	*until last January*
hanggang ka<u>ha</u>pon	*until yesterday*
hanggang ngayon	*until today, up to now*
hanggang <u>bu</u>kas	*until tomorrow*

Combining time expressions

mula' ka<u>ha</u>pon hanggang <u>bu</u>kas	*from yesterday to tomorrow*
mula' ala <u>u</u>na hanggang alas tres	*from one o'clock to three o'clock*

<u>Lu</u>nes ng <u>ha</u>pon	*Monday afternoon*
<u>bu</u>kas ng <u>ha</u>pon	*tomorrow afternoon*
<u>Lu</u>nes ng ala <u>u</u>na	*Monday at one o'clock*
<u>bu</u>kas ng ala <u>u</u>na	*tomorrow at one o'clock*
<u>Lu</u>nes ng ala <u>u</u>na ng <u>ha</u>pon	*Monday at one o'clock in the afternoon*
<u>bu</u>kas ng ala <u>u</u>na ng <u>ha</u>pon	*tomorrow at one o'clock in the afternoon*

ka<u>ni</u>nang <u>ha</u>pon	*this afternoon (earlier today)*
ngayong <u>ha</u>pon	*this afternoon (now, later today)*
<u>ma</u>mayang <u>ha</u>pon	*this afternoon (later today)*

Sentences:

Dumating sila ka<u>ni</u>nang <u>ha</u>pon.	*They arrived this afternoon.* *(It is now the evening.)*
<u>Da</u>rating sila ngayong <u>ha</u>pon.	*They will arrive this afternoon.* *(It is now the afternoon or the* *morning.)*
<u>Da</u>rating sila <u>ma</u>mayang <u>ha</u>pon.	*They will arrive this afternoon.* *(It is now the morning.)*

Time clauses

pag, kapag, pagka, kapagka

when

completed and uncompleted forms	
pag nag-<u>a</u>ral sila	*when they study (in the future)*
pag nag-<u>aa</u>ral sila	*when they are studying*

verbless	
pag ma<u>i</u>nit	*when it's hot*

noong

when

for past actions or situations

often shortened to **nung**

completed, uncompleted and unstarted forms	
noong nag-<u>a</u>ral sila	*when they studied*
noong nag-<u>aa</u>ral sila	*when they were studying*
noong mag-<u>aa</u>ral na sila	*when they were about to study*

verbless	
noong nan<u>di</u>to sila	*when they were here*
noong <u>ba</u>ta' ako	*when I was a child*

pag- and pagka-

when, as soon as

Pag- and **pagka-** can be combined with a root expressing an action to mean *when...*.

pag-alis nila	*when they leave/left*
pagkaalis nila	*when they have/had left* *after they leave/left*
pagbalik nila	*when they return/returned*
pagkabalik nila	*when they have/had returned* *after they return/returned*

The word starting with **pag-/pagka-** can be repeated to mean *as soon as…*. **Na/-ng** (p. 34) is placed after the first **pag-/pagka-** word.

pag-alis *na* pag-alis nila	*as soon as they leave/left*
pagkaalis *na* pagkaalis nila	*as soon as they have/had left*

nang

when, as soon as
for past actions or situations

basic form	
nang mag-a<u>sa</u>wa si John	*when/as soon as John got married*

kung kailan/<u>ke</u>lan…, saka'…

just when
used to say that something has happened at an unsuitable time

completed, uncompleted and unstarted forms	
Kung <u>ke</u>lan umalis na ako, saka' sila tu<u>ma</u>wag.	*Just when I had left, they called.*
Kung <u>ke</u>lan nag<u>ta</u>tra<u>ba</u>ho ako, saka' sila tu<u>ma</u>wag.	*Just when I was working, they called.*
Kung <u>ke</u>lan <u>a</u>alis ako, saka' sila tu<u>ma</u>wag.	*Just when I was going to leave, they called.*

Kung <u>ke</u>lan busy ako, saka' sila tu<u>ma</u>wag.	*Just when I was busy, they called.*
Kung <u>ke</u>lan paalis na ako, saka' sila tu<u>ma</u>wag.*	*Just when I was about to leave, they called.*

* See also: **pa-** ² (p. 253)

<u>o</u>ras na

the minute
for future actions or situations
often used for warnings and threats

basic form	
<u>o</u>ras na dumating sila	*the minute they arrive*

verbless	
<u>o</u>ras na nan<u>di</u>to sila	*the minute they are here*

mula' nang, mula' noong

since, after
also: **magmula' nang, magmula' noong**

basic form	
mula' noong mag-a<u>sa</u>wa si Mary	*since/after Mary got married*
mula' noong maging presi<u>de</u>nte si Mandela	*since/after Mandela became president*

mula' noong nag-a<u>sa</u>wa si Mary	*since/after Mary got married*

mula' noong <u>ba</u>ta' si Mary	*since Mary was a child*

<u>ha</u>bang
while

<u>ha</u>bang nag-<u>aa</u>ral sila	*while they are studying* *while they were studying*

<u>ha</u>bang nan<u>di</u>to si Fred	*while Fred is here*

saman<u>ta</u>la' -ng
while

saman<u>ta</u>la*ng* nag-<u>aa</u>ral sila	*while they are studying* *while they were studying*

| samanta**la**ng nan**di**to si Fred | *while Fred is here* |

See also: **Na/-ng** (p. 34)

hanggang sa
until

basic form	
hanggang sa mag-a̱ral sila	*until they study* *until they studied*

completed form	
hanggang sa nag-a̱ral sila	*until they studied*

tuwing
every time

uncompleted and unstarted forms	
tuwing nag-a̱aral sila **tuwing mag-a̱aral sila**	*every time they study*

verbless	
tuwing nandi**to sila**	*every time they're here*

bago
before

bago sila mag-aral	*before they study* *before they studied* *before studying*
bago mag-ala-una	*before one o'clock*
bago maging presidente si Mandela	*before Mandela becomes president* *before Mandela became president*

completed form

bago sila nag-aral	*before they studied*

pagkatapos (-ng)
after

basic form

pagkatapos nilang mag-aral **pagkatapos nila mag-aral**	*after they study* *after they studied* *after studying*

See also: **Na/-ng** (p. 34)

Expressing condition

kung

if, when

basic form	
kung mag-<u>a</u>ral sila	*if they study* *when they study*

completed, uncompleted and unstarted forms	
kung nag-<u>a</u>ral sila	*if they studied* *if they had studied*
kung nag-<u>aa</u>ral sila	*if they are studying* *if they had been studying*
kung mag-<u>aa</u>ral sila	*if they will study* *if they would study*

verbless	
kung ma<u>i</u>nit	*if it's hot* *if it were hot*
kung nan<u>di</u>to si Fred	*if Fred is here* *if Fred were here*
kung may <u>pe</u>ra ako	*if I have money* *if I had money*

kung sa<u>ka</u>li' -ng

in case

basic form	
kung sa<u>ka</u>li*ng* mag-<u>a</u>ral sila	*in case they study*

completed, uncompleted and unstarted forms	
kung sa<u>ka</u>li*ng* nag-<u>a</u>ral sila	*in case they studied*
kung sa<u>ka</u>li*ng* nag-<u>aa</u>ral sila	*in case they are studying*
kung sa<u>ka</u>li*ng* mag-<u>aa</u>ral sila	*in case they will study*

verbless	
kung sa<u>ka</u>li*ng* ma<u>i</u>nit	*in case it's hot*

See also: **Na/-ng** (p. 34)

hangga't

as long as

uncompleted form	
hangga't nag-<u>aa</u>ral sila	*as long as they are studying*

verbless	
hangga't nan<u>di</u>to si Fred	*as long as Fred is here*

basta't

as long as

completed, uncompleted and unstarted forms	
basta't nag-<u>a</u>ral sila	*as long as they studied*
basta't nag-<u>aa</u>ral sila	*as long as they are studying*
basta't mag-<u>aa</u>ral sila	*as long as they will study*

verbless	
basta't nan<u>di</u>to si Fred	*as long as Fred is here*

ngayon -ng... na

now that

completed, uncompleted and unstarted forms	
ngayong nag-<u>a</u>ral na sila	*now that they have studied*
ngayong nag-<u>aa</u>ral na sila	*now that they are studying*
ngayong mag-<u>aa</u>ral na sila	*now that they will study*

verbless	
ngayong nan<u>di</u>to na sila	*now that they are here*

See also: **Na/-ng** (p. 34)

pwera na lang kung, maliban na lang kung

unless

also: pwera kung, maliban kung

basic form

pwera na lang kung mag-aral sila	*unless they study*

completed, uncompleted and unstarted forms

pwera na lang kung nag-aral sila	*unless they studied*
pwera na lang kung nag-aaral sila	*unless they are studying*
pwera na lang kung mag-aaral sila	*unless they study*

verbless

pwera na lang kung nandito sila	*unless they are here* *unless they were here*

kung hindi' lang

if it weren't for / if it hadn't been for (the fact that)
also: **kung hindi' (nga') lang (sana)**

completed, uncompleted and unstarted forms	
kung hindi' lang sila nag-aral	*if it weren't for the fact that they studied*
kung hindi' lang sila nag-aaral	*if it weren't for the fact that they are studying*
kung hindi' lang sila mag-aaral	*if it weren't for the fact that they will study*

verbless	
kung hindi' lang mahal	*if it weren't (for the fact that it's) expensive*

Expressing cause, result or purpose

dahil, gawa' ng

because

completed, uncompleted and unstarted forms	
dahil nag-aral sila	*because they studied*
dahil nag-aaral sila	*because they are studying* *because they were studying*
dahil mag-aaral sila	*because they will study*

da̲hil nan̲d̲ito sila	*because they are here*
	because they were here

da̲hil sa

because of

da̲hil sa b̲a̲ta'	*because of the child*
da̲hil kay John	*because of John*
da̲hil sa iyo	*because of you*

See also: Sa phrase (p. 70)

porke

just because

porke nag-a̲ral sila	*just because they studied*
porke nag-a̲a̲ral sila	*just because they are studying*
	just because they were studying
porke mag-a̲a̲ral sila	*just because they will study*

porke nan<u>di</u>to sila	*just because they are here*
	just because they were here

kaya'

that's why, so

kaya' nag-<u>a</u>ral sila	*that's why they studied*
kaya' nag-<u>aa</u>ral sila	*that's why they are studying*
	that's why they were studying
kaya' mag-<u>aa</u>ral sila	*that's why they will study*

kaya' nan<u>di</u>to sila	*that's why they are here*
	that's why they were here

p<u>a</u>ra

so that, in order to

p<u>a</u>ra mag-<u>a</u>ral sila	*so that they'll study*
p<u>a</u>ra mag-<u>a</u>ral	*(in order) to study*

verbless	
p<u>a</u>ra nan<u>di</u>to sila	*so that they're here*
	so that they'll be here

p<u>a</u>ra sa

for

noun, pronoun	
p<u>a</u>ra sa <u>b</u>ata'	*for the child*
p<u>a</u>ra kay John	*for John*
p<u>a</u>ra sa iyo	*for you*

See also: Sa phrase (p. 70)

<u>a</u>lang-<u>a</u>lang sa

for the sake of

noun, pronoun	
<u>a</u>lang-<u>a</u>lang sa <u>b</u>ata'	*for the sake of the child*
<u>a</u>lang-<u>a</u>lang kay John	*for John's sake*
<u>a</u>lang-<u>a</u>lang sa iyo	*for your sake*

See also: Sa phrase (p. 70)

at nang

so that

basic form	
at nang mag-<u>a</u>ral sila	*so that they'll study*
at nang pumayat sila	*so that they'll lose weight*

verbless	
at nang nan<u>di</u>to sila	*so that they're here* *so that they'll be here*

Expressing contrast

<u>ka</u>hit, maski

even though, even if
also: <u>ka</u>hit na, maski na

basic form – for hypothetical future actions or situations	
<u>ka</u>hit na mag-<u>a</u>ral ka	*even if you study*

completed, uncompleted and unstarted forms – for actual actions or situations *("despite the fact that")*

ka̲hit na nag-a̲ral sila	*even though they studied*
ka̲hit na nag-aa̲ral sila	*even though they are studying* *even though they were studying*
ka̲hit na mag-aa̲ral sila	*even though they will study*

verbless

ka̲hit na nandi̲to sila	*even if/though they are here* *even if/though they were here*

Note: **ka̲hit (na) / maski (na)** can also mean *even*.

ka̲hit ngayon	*even now*
ka̲hit si John	*even John*

imbes na, sa halip na
instead of

basic form

imbes na mag-a̲ral	*instead of studying*

pwera sa, maliban sa

except (for)

noun, pronoun	
pwera sa bata'	*except the child*
pwera kay John	*except John*
maliban sa iyo	*except you*

See also: Sa phrase (p. 70)

Expressing possibility

baka

maybe, might

basic form – *might, I'm afraid*	
Baka mag-aral sila.	*They might study.*
Baka mahulog sila.	*They might fall.* *I'm afraid they might fall.*

completed, uncompleted and unstarted forms – *maybe, might*	
Baka nag-aral sila.	*Maybe they studied.*
Baka nag-aaral sila.	*Maybe they are studying.* *Maybe they were studying.*
Baka mag-aaral sila.	*Maybe they will study.*

| Baka nan<u>di</u>to sila. | *Maybe they are here.* |
| | *Maybe they were here.* |

baka sa<u>ka</u>li' -ng

there's a chance that, perhaps

basic form

| Baka sa<u>ka</u>ling mag-<u>a</u>ral sila. | *There's a chance that they might study.* |
| Baka sa<u>ka</u>ling ma<u>na</u>lo sila. | *There's a chance that they might win.* |

completed, uncompleted and unstarted forms

Baka sa<u>ka</u>ling nag-<u>a</u>ral sila.	*There's a chance that they studied.*
Baka sa<u>ka</u>ling nag-<u>aa</u>ral sila.	*There's a chance that they are studying.*
	There's a chance that they were studying.
Baka sa<u>ka</u>ling mag-<u>aa</u>ral sila.	*There's a chance that they will study.*

verbless	
Baka sak<u>a</u>ling nan<u>di</u>to sila.	*There's a chance that they are here.* *There's a chance that they were here.*

See also: **Na/-ng** (p. 34)

siguro

maybe

completed, uncompleted and unstarted forms	
Sig<u>u</u>ro nag-<u>a</u>ral sila.	*Maybe they studied.*
Sig<u>u</u>ro nag-<u>aa</u>ral sila.	*Maybe they are studying.* *Maybe they were studying.*
Sig<u>u</u>ro mag-<u>aa</u>ral sila.	*Maybe they will study.*

verbless	
Sig<u>u</u>ro nan<u>di</u>to sila.	*Maybe they are here.* *Maybe they were here.*

mukha' -ng, para -ng

it seems, seems (to be/like/that)

completed, uncompleted and unstarted forms	
Mukhang nag-aral sila.	*It seems (that) they studied.*
Mukhang nag-aaral sila.	*It seems (that) they are studying.* *It seems (that) they were studying.*
Mukhang mag-aaral sila.	*It seems (that) they will study.*

verbless	
Mukhang nandito sila.	*It seems (that) they are here.* *It seems (that) they were here.*

See also: **Na/-ng** (p. 34)

malamang

probably, chances are

completed, uncompleted and unstarted forms	
Malamang nag-aral sila.	*They probably studied.*
Malamang nag-aaral sila.	*They are probably studying.* *They were probably studying.*
Malamang mag-aaral sila.	*They will probably study.*

Malamang nan<u>di</u>to sila.	*They are probably here.* *They were probably here.*

sigu<u>ra</u>do -ng, tiyak na

surely, certainly

Sigu<u>ra</u>dong nag-<u>a</u>ral sila.	*They surely studied.*
Sigu<u>ra</u>dong nag-<u>aa</u>ral sila.	*They are surely studying.* *They were surely studying.*
Sigu<u>ra</u>dong mag-<u>aa</u>ral sila.	*They will surely study.*

Sigu<u>ra</u>dong nan<u>di</u>to sila.	*They are surely here.* *They were surely here.*

See also: **Na/-ng** (p. 34)

Expressing other relationships

bukod sa

apart from, besides

noun, pronoun	
bukod sa <u>ba</u>ta'	*apart from the child*
bukod kay John	*apart from John*
bukod sa iyo	*apart from you*

See also: Sa phrase (p. 70)

nang hindi', nang wala'

without (doing, having etc.)

uncompleted form	
nang hindi' nag-<u>aa</u>ral	*without studying*
nang hindi' na<u>papa</u>god	*without getting tired*
nang hindi' na<u>kiki</u>ta' si John	*without seeing John*

verbless	
Ma<u>hi</u>rap ma<u>bu</u>hay nang walang <u>pe</u>ra.	*It's hard to live without money.*
Ma<u>hi</u>rap mag<u>a</u>lit nang walang dahilan.	*It's hard to get angry without any reason.*

tungkol sa

about (on the subject of)

noun, pronoun	
tungkol sa <u>ba</u>ta'	*about the child*
tungkol kay John	*about John*
tungkol sa iyo	*about you*

See also: Sa phrase (p. 70)

uli', ulit

again

completed, uncompleted and unstarted forms	
Nag-<u>a</u>ral sila ulit.	*They studied again.*
Nag-<u>aa</u>ral sila ulit.	*They are studying again.* *They were studying again.*
Mag-<u>aa</u>ral sila ulit.	*They will study again.*

verbless	
Nan<u>di</u>to sila ulit.	*They are here again.* *They were here again.*

talaga (-ng)

really

completed, uncompleted and unstarted forms	
Talagang nag-aral sila.	*They really studied.*
Talagang nag-aaral sila.	*They are really studying.* *They were really studying.*
Talagang mag-aaral sila.	*They will really study.*

verbless	
Talagang nandito sila.	*They are really here.* *They were really here.*

See also: **Na/-ng** (p. 34)

halos

almost, nearly

basic form	
Halos mahulog si John.	*John almost fell.*

verbless	
halos lahat	*almost all*

muntik na (-ng), kamuntik na (-ng)

almost, nearly

basic form	
Muntik nang ma<u>hu</u>log si John.	*John almost fell.*

See also: **Na/-ng** (p. 34)

l<u>a</u>lo (-ng)

even (more)

completed, uncompleted and unstarted forms	
L<u>a</u>long lumakas ang bagyo.	*The typhoon became even stronger.*
L<u>a</u>long lum<u>a</u>lakas ang bagyo.	*The typhoon is becoming even stronger.* *The typhoon was becoming even stronger.*
L<u>a</u>long l<u>a</u>lakas ang bagyo.	*The typhoon will become even stronger.*

See also: **Na/-ng** (p. 34)

lalo na

especially

lalo na si John	*especially John*
lalo na sa Maynila'	*especially in Manila*

sa madaling salita'

in short

Sa madaling salita', nanalo sila.	*In short, they won.*

sa bandang huli

in the end

Sa bandang huli, nanalo sila.	*In the end, they won.*

sa wakas

finally, at last

Sa wakas, nanalo sila!	*At last, they won!*

Enclitic words

Overview

In Tagalog, enclitic words are words that generally follow either the first word of the sentence or another enclitic word.

The following words are enclitic:

- Ang personal pronouns*, i.e. **ako, ka, siya, kami, tayo, kayo, sila**
- Ng personal pronouns, i.e. **ko, mo, niya, namin, natin, ninyo, nila**
- the pronoun **kita**
- the particles **na, pa, man, nga', din/rin, lang, naman, daw/raw, po', ho', ba, pala, kaya', muna, tuloy, kasi, yata', sana**

Examples:

Kumain *sila* ng kanin.	*They ate rice.*
Kumain *rin sila* ng kanin.	*They also ate rice.*

* Ang personal pronouns are only enclitic when used as the POD (p. 35) of the sentence. When used as the News (p. 35), an Ang personal pronoun is usually the first word of the sentence. Example:

Sila ang ku<u>ma</u>in ng <u>ka</u>nin.	*They were the ones who ate (the) rice.*

See also:

- Ang personal pronouns (p. 53)
- Ng personal pronouns (p. 58)
- **Kita** (p. 71)
- Verbs, adjectives etc. used as nouns (p. 101)

Using enclitic words

Enclitic words and na/-ng

If the first word of a sentence requires a **na/-ng**, the **na/-ng** is inserted after any enclitic words in the sentence. Examples:

Wala*ng* <u>pe</u>ra si Juan.	*Juan has no money.*
Wala' siya*ng* <u>pe</u>ra.	*He/she has no money.*
Wala' rin siya*ng* <u>pe</u>ra.	*He/she has no money either.*

See also:

- **Na/-ng** (p. 34)
- **May, mayroon/<u>me</u>ron, ma<u>ra</u>mi, wala'** (p. 379)

Order of enclitic words

When there are two or more enclitic words in a sentence, they generally appear in the following order:

1	2			3	4
ka	na/pa	naman	pala	niya	ako
ko	man	daw/raw	kaya'	namin	siya
mo	nga'	po'/ho'	muna	natin	kami
	din/rin	ba	tuloy	ninyo	tayo
	lang		kasi	nila	kayo
			yata'		sila
			sana	kita	

Note: Enclitic particles (column 2) are generally used in the order given above, i.e. **na** comes before **man**, **lang** before **naman** etc.

Examples:

Nakita' ko sila.	*I saw them.*
Nakita' nila ako.	*They saw me.*
Nakita' rin kita.	*I saw you too.*
Nakita' rin yata' nila ako.	*Maybe they saw me too.*
Nakita' ka rin yata' nila.	*Maybe they saw you too.*

Enclitic words in clauses or Ang/Ng/Sa phrases

If an enclitic word is a part of a clause, it follows the first word of the clause. Example:

Dahil gutom si Alfred, ku<u>ma</u>in *siya* **ng <u>ka</u>nin.**	*Because Alfred was hungry, he ate some rice.*

If an enclitic word is a part of an Ang/Ng/Sa phrase (p. 70), it follows the word after **ang/ng/sa**. Example:

Ito ang ki<u>na</u>in *niya* **ka<u>ha</u>pon.**	*This is what he/she ate yesterday.*

See also: Verbs, adjectives etc. used as nouns (p. 101)

Exceptions to the follow-the-first-word rule

1. Enclitic words cannot immediately follow any of the words below. Instead, they follow the word after them.

- markers, i.e. **ang, kay, kina, ni, nina, ng, sa, si, sina**
- **ay, e di', <u>ha</u>los, kaysa, mas, may, mga, <u>na</u> kay, <u>na</u> kina, <u>na</u>sa**
- the verb **maging** and its different forms
- **at, at saka, bukod, <u>da</u>hil, <u>ha</u>bang, hanggang, hangga't, imbes na, kapag, kapagka, kung, kung sa<u>ka</u>li', ma<u>li</u>ban, mula', nang, noon, o,**

o kaya', pag, pagka, pero, porke, sa halip na, samantalang, tuwing, sakali'

Example:

| Dahil gutom *sila*, kinain nila ang kanin.* | *Because they were hungry, they ate the rice.* |

* **Sila** cannot immediately follow **dahil**.

Note: Enclitic particles except **na** and **pa** may immediately follow **dahil** and **halos**. All enclitic particles may immediately follow **bukod, kung sakali', maliban, mula', noon** and **sakali'**.

2. Enclitic words cannot immediately follow the first word of the phrases below. Instead, they follow the entire phrase.

* names such as Mario Cruz
* numbers and expressions that include numbers such as **dalawa at kalahati'** *(two and a half)*, **limang taon** *(five years)*
* dates, addresses, times of day
* repeated words such as **magandang maganda**
* some describing words

Example:

| **Si Mario Cruz *siya*.*** | *He is Mario Cruz.* |

* **Siya** cannot immediately follow **si** or **Mario**.

3. Enclitic words may, but do not have to, immediately follow the words below.

- baka, <u>ba</u>kit, <u>ga</u>ling, <u>ga</u>ya, mukha', <u>pa</u>ra, tungkol
- tig- + number
- some describing words
- the first word in describing phrases such as <u>bu</u>kas ng <u>ha</u>pon

Examples:

<u>Ba</u>kit *sila* umalis? <u>Ba</u>kit umalis *sila*?	*Why did they leave?*
Tiglilima *sila*ng candy. Tiglilimang candy *sila*.	*They have/get/got/etc. five candies each.*
<u>Ba</u>go *ko*ng account ito. <u>Ba</u>gong account *ko* ito.	*This is my new account.*
<u>Bu</u>kas *sila* ng <u>ha</u>pon <u>a</u>alis. <u>Bu</u>kas ng <u>ha</u>pon *sila* <u>a</u>alis.	*They will leave tomorrow afternoon.*
<u>Pa</u>ra *siya*ng si Fred. <u>Pa</u>rang si Fred *siya*.	*He's like Fred.*

Note: **Na** and **pa** cannot immediately follow <u>ba</u>kit.

Meanings of enclitic particles

Na

na [1]

now, already

Member na ako.	*I'm now a member.*
Ku<u>mai</u>n ka na. (basic form)	*Eat now.*
Ku<u>mai</u>n na ako. (completed form)	*I already ate.* *I have/had (already) eaten.*
Ku<u>maka</u>in na ako.	*I'm eating now.*
<u>Kaka</u>in na ako.	*I'll eat now.* *I'm about to eat.*

Wala' nang mangga.	*There are no more mangoes.* Lit. *no mangoes now*
Hindi' na member si Fred.	*Fred is not a member anymore.* Lit. *not a member now*
Hindi' na nag<u>tata</u>go' si John.	*John isn't hiding anymore.* Lit. *doesn't hide now*
Hindi' na mag<u>tata</u>go' si John.	*John won't hide anymore.* Lit. *won't hide now*
Huwag ka nang mag<u>ta</u>go'.	*Don't hide anymore.* Lit. *don't hide now*

Alas kwatro na.	It's four o'clock.
Tanghali' na.	It's noon.
Pasko na!	It's Christmas!

See also: Aspects (p. 206)

na [2]

already (so soon)

Aalis ka na?	Are you leaving already? (So soon?)

na [3]

finally (after a while, after some difficulty, or when a certain condition is met); unlike before

Pwede na akong umalis.	I can finally leave.

na [4]

after all; instead of other options; instead of what has been said or planned before or what is expected

Bukas ka na umalis.	Leave tomorrow instead.
Sasama na ako.	I'll come along after all.
Ako na ang magluluto'.	I'll do the cooking (instead of you; leave it to me).

time expression + na

starting..., from... onwards

<u>Pwe</u>de na akong umalis <u>bu</u>kas.	*I can leave starting tomorrow.*

future time expression + na

as early as (used to imply that it's so soon or too soon)

<u>Bu</u>kas na ang exam.	*The exam is (as early as) tomorrow.* *(And I haven't studied yet.)*
Next week na ang kasal!	*The wedding is (as early as) next week!* *(It's now only one week till the wedding!)*

pag... na

once, when (from the time that)

<u>Tata</u>wag ako pag tapos na ang palabas.	*I'll call once the show is finished (from the time that it's finished).*

verb expressing ability in completed form + na

has (ever)

Nakapunta na ako sa Cebu.	*I've been to Cebu.*
Nakapunta ka na ba sa Cebu?	*Have you (ever) been to Cebu?*

See also: Verbs expressing ability at **ma-** (p. 136), **maka-** [1], **makapag-**, **makapang-** (p. 166) and **mapa-** (p. 180).

hindi' na... kahit kailan

will never again

Hindi' na ako magsisigarilyo kahit kailan.	*I'll never smoke again.*

kahit na, maski na [1]

even though, even if

kahit na mag-aral ka	*even if you study*
kahit na nag-aral sila	*even though they studied*
kahit na nandito sila	*even if/though they are here* *even if/though they were here*

See also: **Kahit, maski** (p. 326)

kahit na, maski na [2]

even

kahit ngayon	*even now*
kahit si John	*even John*

na lang [1]

after all; instead of other options; instead of what has been said or planned before or what is expected

Bukas ka na lang umalis.	*Leave tomorrow instead.*

na lang [2]

just

Magkita' na lang tayo bukas.	*Let's just see each other tomorrow.*

na lang [3]

used when stating what you have picked out of two or more options

Kape na lang.	*Coffee.* (when offered coffee or tea)

na naman

again

Late na naman sila.	*They're late again.*
Brownout na naman?!	*Blackout again?!*

... na, ... pa [1]

what's more, on top of that, not only...

Maganda na, matalino pa.	*She's pretty, and what's more, she's smart.*
Pangit na, masungit pa.	*He/she's ugly, and what's more, he/she's bad-tempered.*
Nadulas na, pinagtawanan pa.	*He/she slipped, and what's more, he/she got laughed at.*

... na, ... pa [2]

(already)... but still

Matanda' na, malakas pa.	*He/she's (already) old but still strong.*

(kahit na)... na, ... pa rin

even though/if..., still

Luma' na, gumagana pa rin. Kahit na luma' na, gumagana pa rin.	*Even though it's old, it still works.*

na rin
as well

Linisin mo na rin ito.	*Clean this as well.*

na rin lang
since... anyway

Nandito ka na rin lang, bakit hindi' ka kumain dito?	*Since you're here anyway, why don't you eat here?*

ngayon -ng... na
now that

ngayong nag-aral na sila	*now that they have studied*
ngayong nandito na sila	*now that they are here*

See also: **Ngayon -ng... na** (p. 320)

pwera na lang kung, maliban na lang kung

unless

pwera na lang kung mag-aral sila	*unless they study*
pwera na lang kung nag-aral sila	*unless they studied*
pwera na lang kung nandito sila	*unless they are here* *unless they were here*

See also: Pwera na lang kung, maliban na lang kung (p. 321)

Other sentences and phrases:

Ako na.	*Let me do it.*
Bahala' na.	*We'll see. / I'll let things take their course.*
Di' bale na lang.	*Never mind. / Oh well.*
Huwag na.	*Never mind (don't do that). Don't bother.*
Pasensya na.	*Sorry.*
Pwede na.	*It's good enough.*
Pwede na 'yan.	*That's good enough.*
Sabi ko na nga' ba.	*I knew it all along. I told you (so).*
saka' na (lang)	*some other time, (for) another time*

Sige na...	Come on, please... (used for asking someone to do something)
Tara na.	Let's go.

See also:

- ... pa lang, ... na (p. 356)
- ... pa, ... na (p. 356)

Pa

pa

still, yet, in addition, more, even

Member pa ako.	I'm still a member.
Ku<u>mai</u>n ka pa. (basic form)	Eat some more.
Ku<u>mai</u>n pa ako. (completed form)	I also ate. (I ate as well as did other things.)
Ku<u>makai</u>n pa ako.	I'm still eating.
<u>Kakai</u>n pa ako.	I'll eat some more. I'll also eat. (I'll eat as well as do other things.)
Wala' pang mangga.	There are no mangoes yet. Lit. still no mangoes
Hindi' pa member si Fred.	Fred isn't a member yet. Lit. still not a member

Hindi' pa ku<u>maka</u>in si Fred.	*Fred hasn't eaten yet.* Lit. *still hasn't eaten*
Hindi' pa <u>kaka</u>in si Fred.	*Fred won't be eating yet.* Lit. *still won't eat*

Isa pa.	*One more.*
<u>Si</u>no pa ang <u>da</u>rating?	*Who else is coming?* Lit. *who in addition*
Mas malaki pa.	*Even bigger.*

See also: Aspects (p. 206)

future time expression + pa

not until (used to imply that it's still some time away)

<u>Bu</u>kas pa ang exam.	*The exam is (not until)* *tomorrow.* *(I still have plenty of time to* *study.)*
Next week pa ang kasal!	*The wedding is (not until) next* *week!* *(It's not tomorrow!)*

past time expression + pa [1]

as long ago as (used to imply that it's already some time ago)

Ka<u>ha</u>pon pa ang deadline.	*The deadline was yesterday.* *(Not today.)*
Noong isang linggo pa ang birthday ko.	*My birthday was last week.* *(Even though we celebrated it yesterday.)*

past time expression + pa [2] / mula' pa

since as long ago as (used to imply that something has been the case since some time ago)

Ka<u>ha</u>pon pa na<u>wa</u>wala' ang libro. **Mula' pa ka<u>ha</u>pon na<u>wa</u>wala' ang libro.**	*The book has been missing since yesterday.* *(And I still haven't found it.)*
Noong isang linggo pa <u>na</u>sa Paris si John. **Mula' pa noong isang linggo <u>na</u>sa Paris si John.**	*John has been in Paris since last week.* *(He's had plenty of time to explore the city.)*

hindi' pa... kahit kailan

has never

Hindi' pa na<u>ka</u>ka<u>bo</u>to si Mark <u>ka</u>hit kailan.	*Mark has never voted.*
Hindi' pa na<u>ka</u>ka<u>ka</u>in ng sushi si Mark <u>ka</u>hit kailan.	*Mark has never eaten sushi.*
Hindi' pa nag<u>ka</u>kabu<u>lu</u>tong si Mark <u>ka</u>hit kailan.	*Mark has never had chicken pox.*

pa lang

only, just

January pa lang.	*It's only January.*

... pa lang, ... na

only/just... but... already

May pa lang, may bagyo na.	*It's only May but there's already a typhoon.*

... pa, ... na

still... but... already

Ma<u>a</u>ga pa, madilim na.	*It's still early but it's already dark.*
<u>Ba</u>ta' pa, mature na.	*He/she's still young but already mature.*

pa rin

still

U<u>muu</u>lan pa rin.	*It's still raining.*

Other sentences and phrases:

Ako pa!	*Of course, I can/could do that!*
Si John pa!	*Of course, John can/could do that!*

See also:

- ... na, ... pa [1] (p. 350)
- ... na, ... pa [2] (p. 350)
- (<u>ka</u>hit na)... na, ... pa rin (p. 350)
- pa kasi (p. 375)

Man

... man o...

whether... or...

<u>Ka</u>hit <u>si</u>no <u>pwe</u>deng su<u>ma</u>li', <u>ba</u>ta' man o matanda'.	*Anyone can join, whether young or old.*

hindi' man lang

not even

Hindi' man lang tum<u>a</u>wag si John.	*John didn't even call.*

wala' man lang

no one even, nothing even

Wala' man lang dumating.	*No one even came.*

Nga'

nga' [1]

indeed, really, sure enough, in fact

<u>O</u>o nga'.	*Yes, that's right.* *Yes, indeed.*
Totoo nga'.	*It's really true.*
M<u>u</u>ra nga'.	*Sure enough, it's cheap.*

nga' [2]

used to express mild irritation or impatience

Sige na nga'.	*Oh, all right.* (expressing reluctance)
Kumain ka nga'!	*Come on! Eat!*
Alis nga'!	*Leave!*
Huwag ka ngang kumain!	*Don't eat!*

nga' [3]

used to make a command or a request more polite and friendly, or for emphasis

Kumain ka nga' ng isda'.	*Please just eat some fish.*
Paabot nga' ng isda'. **Pakiabot nga' ng isda'.**	*Could you just pass the fish, please.*

See also: Commands, requests and wishes (p. 220)

nga' [4]

used to challenge someone to prove that they can do what they say they can do

Mag-split ka nga'!	*Do the splits! (Show me!)*

basic form + nga'

why don't

Ku<u>ma</u>in nga' <u>ta</u>yo.	*Why don't we eat.*
Ta<u>wa</u>gan nga' <u>na</u>tin siya.	*Why don't we call him/her.*
Maghintay nga' sila.	*Why don't they wait.*

(<u>sa</u>na), ... nga' lang

but, only

Maganda (<u>sa</u>na) siya, bastos nga' lang.	*She's pretty, but she's rude.*

... nga', ... naman

... all right, but...

Maganda nga', bastos naman.	*She's pretty all right, but she's rude.*
Mahal nga', ma<u>ti</u>bay naman.	*It's expensive all right, but it's sturdy.*

'yun nga' lang

the only thing is, the only problem is

Maganda ang bag. 'Yun nga' lang, mahal.	*The bag is nice. The only thing is, it's expensive.*

Other sentences and phrases:

A<u>yo</u>ko nga'!	*I don't like/want it! I don't like/want to! I'm not interested! No way!*
<u>Bu</u>ti nga' (sa 'yo/sa kanila/etc).	*It serves you/them/etc. right.*
<u>O</u>o nga' naman.	*That's true. You've/he's/etc. got a point.*
<u>O</u>o nga' pala.	*Oh yes, that's right (I'd forgotten about that).*
<u>o</u>o nga' pala... siya nga' pala...	*by the way...*
Sige nga'!	*If you can really do it, show me!*

See also:

* **kung hindi' (nga') lang (<u>sa</u>na)** (p. 363)
* **<u>Sa</u>bi ko na nga' ba.** (p. 352)

Din/Rin

din/rin [1]

too, also, either

Maganda rin si Maria.	*Maria is pretty too.*
Hindi' rin maganda si Maria.	*Maria isn't pretty either.*

din/rin ²

finally, at last

Natupad rin ang pa<u>nga</u>rap ko.	*My dream finally came true.*

din/rin ³

fairly, not very, (good/big/etc.) enough

A: **Malaki ba ang <u>ba</u>hay?** B: **<u>O</u>o, malaki rin.**	A: *Is the house big?* B: *Yes, it's big enough. (It's not that big.)*

See also:

- **(<u>ka</u>hit na)... na, ... pa rin** (p. 350)
- **na rin** (p. 351)
- **na rin lang** (p. 351)
- **pa rin** (p. 357)

Lang

Note: The formal way of saying **lang** is **<u>la</u>mang**.

lang

only, just

Dalawa lang.	*Just two.*
Ka<u>ha</u>pon lang.	*Just yesterday.*

verb in recently completed form + lang

just

<u>Ka</u>kaalis lang nila.	*They just left.*

See also: Aspects (p. 206), Recently completed form (p. 215)

(<u>sa</u>na)... kaya' lang / <u>ka</u>so lang

the only thing is, the only problem is

Maganda (<u>sa</u>na) ang bag. Kaya' lang mahal.	*The bag is nice. The only thing is, it's expensive.*

kung hindi' (nga') lang (<u>sa</u>na)

if it weren't (for the fact that)

kung hindi' lang sila nag-<u>a</u>ral	*if it weren't for the fact that they studied*
kung hindi' lang mahal	*if it weren't (for the fact that it's) expensive*

See also: **Kung hindi' lang** (p. 322)

kung... lang s<u>a</u>na

if only

Kung naghintay lang <u>sa</u>na ako.	*If only I had waited.*
Kung ginawa' ko lang <u>sa</u>na iyon.	*If only I had done that.*
Kung ma<u>ya</u>man lang <u>sa</u>na ako.	*If only I were rich.*

Other sentences and phrases:

<u>Bi</u>ro' lang. Joke lang.	*Just kidding.*
sa totoo lang	*if truth be told* *to be honest*
<u>Te</u>ka lang.	*Wait a minute.*
Wala' lang.	*It doesn't matter. It's nothing.*

See also:

- **Di' ba̲le na lang.** (p. 352)
- **hindi' man lang** (p. 358)
- **na lang** [1] (p. 349)
- **na lang** [2] (p. 349)
- **na lang** [3] (p. 349)
- **na rin lang** (p. 351)
- **(sa̲na), ... nga' lang** (p. 360)
- **pa lang** (p. 356)
- **... pa lang, ... na** (p. 356)
- **pwe̲ra na lang kung, mali̲ban na lang kung** (p. 352)
- **saka' na (lang)** (p. 352)
- **wala' man lang** (p. 358)
- **'yun nga' lang** (p. 360)

Naman

naman [1]

used to show contrast between two persons, things or ideas

Mahi̲lig si John sa kape, si Mary naman sa tsaa.	*John likes coffee, while Mary likes tea.*
Kaha̲pon si John. Ngayon naman si Mary.	*Yesterday, it was John. Today, it's Mary.*

naman [2]

used to show contrast with what usually happens, what has recently or just happened, or what might be expected

Ku<u>ma</u>in naman <u>ta</u>yo sa labas.	*Let's eat out for a change.*
Ikaw naman ang mag<u>lu</u>to'.	*You do the cooking this time. It's your turn to cook.*
Mag-<u>a</u>ral ka naman.	*Why don't you study (for a change).*
Ak<u>o</u> naman!	*Hey, it's my turn!*

naman [3]

used to show contrast with what someone said, for instance, when expressing an opposing opinion or correcting someone

Mabait naman siya.	*He/she's actually nice.*
Hindi' naman siya buntis.	*Actually, she's not pregnant.*

naman [4]

used to soften what is said, or to make it less direct or less definite

Ma<u>bu</u>ti naman.	*Fine (not very good but not very bad either).*
Hindi' naman.	*Not really.*

naman [5]

used to make a command or a request more polite and friendly, or for emphasis

Ku<u>mai</u>n ka naman.	*Please just eat.*
Huwag ka namang ku<u>mai</u>n.	*Please just don't eat.*
Paabot naman ng isda'. Pakiabot naman ng isda'.	*Could you just pass the fish, please.*

See also: Commands, requests and wishes (p. 220)

naman [6]

used for introducing a topic that is related to what has just been said

Kumusta si John? ... Kumusta naman ang ne<u>go</u>syo niya?	*How's John? ... And how's his business?*

naman [7]

used to express surprise, admiration, irritation, impatience, disgust, sympathy or other emotions

Ang mahal naman!	*How expensive!*
Ang ta<u>li</u>no mo naman.	*You're really so smart.*
Ka<u>di</u>ri' naman!	*How gross!*
Ka<u>wa</u>wa' ka naman.	*Poor you.*
Mag-<u>a</u>ral ka naman!	*Why don't you study!*
<u>O</u>o naman.	*Of course.*

Other sentences and phrases:

Huwag naman.	*Please don't.*
	Please don't do/say that.
Huwag naman <u>sa</u>na.	*I hope that doesn't happen.*

See also:

- **Kaya' (naman) pala.** (p. 371)
- **na naman** (p. 350)
- **... nga', ... naman** (p. 360)
- <u>O</u>**o nga' naman.** (p. 361)

Daw/Raw

daw/raw

he/she/they say, he/she/they said, I've heard, from what I hear

Malaki raw ang <u>ba</u>hay.	*They said the house was big.*
Ano raw ang nang<u>ya</u>ri?	*What did he/she/etc. say happened?*
Masarap daw ang pag<u>ka</u>in doon.	*I've heard the food there is good.*

Po'/Ho'

po'/ho' [1]

used for talking politely to older people, superiors, adult strangers and adult customers

Ka<u>ha</u>pon lang po'.	*Just yesterday.* (polite)
Malaki ho' ang <u>ba</u>hay.	*The house is big.* (polite)

Note: The polite way of saying *yes* is **<u>o</u>po'** or **<u>o</u>ho'**.

po'/ho' [2]

may be used as a response when an older person, a superior, an adult stranger or an adult customer calls you

A: **Marie!** B: **Po'?**	A: *Marie!* B: *Yes?*

Ba

ba

used as an optional question marker

Ku<u>ma</u>in ka na (ba)?	*Have you eaten yet?*
Kailan (ba) ang birthday mo?	*When is your birthday?*

hindi' ba, di ba

isn't it/he/she, aren't they, didn't you, right etc.

German siya, di ba?	*He/she's German, isn't he/she?*
Di ba German siya?	*Isn't he/she German?*

akala' ko ba

I thought (mistakenly)
expresses puzzlement, disappointment, irritation or other emotions

Akala' ko ba, umalis na si John.	*I thought (mistakenly) John had left. (How come he's still here?)*

See also:

• **Sabi ko na nga' ba.** (p. 352)

Pala

pala ¹

used to express mild surprise at new or unexpected information

Ikaw pala si Mary!	*Oh, so you're Mary!*
Ang laki pala ng bahay nila!	*I didn't know their house was so big!*

pala [2]

after all (despite what was said or planned before)

Inosente pala siya.	*He/she's innocent after all.*
Tama' pala siya.	*He/she's right after all.*
Hindi' pala kami aalis.	*We're not leaving after all.*

pala [3]

used when adding an extra comment or an afterthought

Pakilinis pala ng kwarto ko.	*By the way, could you clean my room.* *Oh, and could you clean my room.*

Other sentences and phrases:

Kaya' (naman) pala.	*So that's why.*
Kaya' (naman) pala mura.	*So that's why it's cheap.*

See also:

- **Oo nga' pala.** (p. 361)
- **oo nga' pala...** (p. 361)
- **siya nga' pala...** (p. 361)

Kaya'

kaya' [1]

should perhaps

Tu<u>ma</u>wag ka kaya'.	*Perhaps you should call.*
Tu<u>ma</u>wag kaya' <u>ta</u>yo.	*Perhaps we should call.*
Tu<u>ma</u>wag kaya' ako.	*Perhaps I should call.*

kaya' [2]

I wonder, do you think, do you suppose

Mahal kaya'?	*Do you think it's expensive?* *I wonder if it's expensive.*
<u>Si</u>no kaya' ang ma<u>na</u>nalo?	*Who do you suppose will win?* *I wonder who will win.*
Ku<u>ma</u>in na kaya' sila?	*Do you think they've eaten?* *I wonder if they've eaten.*
<u>Ba</u>kit kaya'.	*I wonder why.*

e kung... kaya'

what if

E kung umalis kaya' ako?	*What if I leave?*
	What if I had left?
E kung mag-aral kaya' ako?	*What if I study?*
E kung nag-aral kaya' ako?	*What if I had studied?*

Muna

muna [1]

first

Ako muna!	*Me first!*
Basahin mo muna ito.	*Read this first.*
Kumain ka muna.	*Eat first.*
Teka muna.	*Wait a minute.*
	Lit. *Wait first.*

muna [2]

for the time being, for now, for a while

Iyan lang muna.	*That's all for now.*
	Lit. *Just that for now.*

muna [3]

yet (used in negative commands or requests, e.g. *don't, let's not*)

Huwag ka munang kumain.	*Don't eat yet.*
Huwag muna tayong kumain.	*Let's not eat yet.*
Huwag muna.	*Don't do that yet.*
	Let's not do that yet.

See also: **Huwag** (p. 225)

Tuloy

tuloy

as a result, that's why
often used with **kasi** (p. 375)

Tinawag mo kasi siyang baboy, nagalit tuloy.	*You called him/her a pig, that's why he/she got angry.*

Kasi

kasi [1]

because, that's because

Note: **Kasi** can also be placed at the beginning of a sentence or clause.

Busog pa ako. <u>Kakakain</u> ko lang kasi.	*I'm still full. That's because I just ate.*
Busog pa ako, kasi <u>kakakain</u> ko lang.	*I'm still full because I just ate.*

kasi [2]

used to blame someone or something or to express regret for something that should not have happened
alternative: **pa kasi** (used with a verb)

Ikaw kasi.	*It's because of you.* *(You are to blame.)*
Siya kasi!	*It's because of him/her!* *(It's his/her fault!)*
Ang tamad kasi niya.	*It's because he/she's lazy.* *(He/she should have studied etc.)*
Umalis ka pa kasi.	*It's because you left.* *(You shouldn't have left.)*

Ayan kasi.	It's because of that. (You shouldn't have done that.)
papaano kasi...	it's because (of the fact that)... (I/you/etc. shouldn't have done that. / That shouldn't have happened.)

Yata'

yata'

it seems, perhaps, maybe, I think, I guess, if I remember correctly
used to express that you are not sure whether something is true

Mahal yata'.	It seems expensive. Maybe it's expensive.
Dalawa yata'.	Maybe two.
Seryoso yata' siya.	He/she seems to be serious.

Sana

sana [1]

I hope

Note: **Sana** can also be placed at the beginning of a sentence or clause.

Ma<u>na</u>lo <u>sa</u>na si Pacquiao. **Sa**na ma<u>na</u>lo si Pacquiao.	*I hope Pacquiao wins.*
Na<u>na</u>lo <u>sa</u>na si Pacquiao. **Sa**na na<u>na</u>lo si Pacquiao.	*I hope Pacquiao won.*

sana [2]

would (be/have/like)
used in requests and wishes

Gusto ko <u>sa</u>na ang <u>ko</u>tse.	*I would like (to get) the car.* *I would have wanted/liked (to get) the car.*
Gusto ko <u>sa</u>nang ku<u>ma</u>in.	*I would like to eat.* *I would have wanted/liked to eat.*
Ma<u>kiki</u>ta<u>wa</u>g lang <u>sa</u>na ako.	*I would just like to make a call (if you don't mind).* *I would just like to borrow your phone.*
Kung <u>pwe</u>de <u>sa</u>na...	*If it would be possible...*

Kung binili ko iyon, mayaman na sana ako ngayon.	If I had bought that, I would be rich by now.
Kung naghintay lang sana ako, nakita' ko sana siya.	If only I had waited, I would have seen him/her.

See also: Pseudo-verbs (p. 236), **Maki-** [2] (p. 171)

verb in unstarted form + sana

was thinking of, was planning to

Tatawag sana ako kahapon.	I was thinking of calling yesterday. I was planning to call yesterday.
Tatawag sana ako bukas.	I was thinking of calling tomorrow. I was planning to call tomorrow.

See also:

- **Huwag naman sana.** (p. 368)
- **(sana)... kaya' lang / kaso lang** (p. 363)
- **kung hindi' (nga') lang (sana)** (p. 363)
- **kung... lang sana** (p. 364)
- **(sana), ... nga' lang** (p. 360)

May, mayroon/meron, marami, wala'

Overview

May, mayroon/meron (meron in spoken Tagalog) and marami are used to indicate existence or possession. Wala' indicates non-existence or non-possession.

May... Merong...	There is/are/was/were (a/some)....	has/have/had (a/some)...
Maraming...	There are/were many.... There is/are/was/were a lot of....	has/have/had many... has/have/had a lot of...
Walang...	There is/are/was/were no....	has/have/had no...

Note: Meron, marami and wala' are linked to the existing/non-existing or possessed/non-possessed object by -ng. See also: Na/-ng (p. 34)

Examples:

May aso. **Merong aso.**	*There is a dog.*
May mangga. **Merong mangga.**	*There is a mango.* *There are some mangoes.*
Maraming aso.	*There are many dogs.*
Maraming asukal.	*There's a lot of sugar.*
Walang aso.	*There are no dogs.*

May aso si Alfred. **Merong aso si Alfred.**	*Alfred has a dog.*
May mangga si Alfred. **Merong mangga si Alfred.**	*Alfred has a mango.* *Alfred has some mangoes.*
Maraming aso si Alfred.	*Alfred has many dogs.*
Maraming pera si Alfred.	*Alfred has a lot of money.*
Walang aso si Alfred.	*Alfred has no dogs.* *Alfred doesn't have a dog.*

Note:

May susi' si Fred.	*Fred has a key.*
Na kay Fred ang susi'.*	*Fred has the key.* Lit. *The key is with Fred.*

* See also: **Nasa** (p. 289)

For other uses of **wala'**, see: **Wala' sa, wala' rito** (p. 294)

Stand-alone m<u>e</u>ron/mar<u>a</u>mi/wala'

M<u>e</u>ron, mar<u>a</u>mi and wala' can also stand alone.

M<u>e</u>ron.	*There is/are/was/were (one/some).* *... has/have/had (one/some).*
Mar<u>a</u>mi.	*There are/were many.* *There is/are/was/were a lot.* *... has/have/had many.* *... has/have/had a lot.*
Wala'.	*There is/are/was/were none.* *... has/have/had none.*

Examples:

May <u>a</u>so ba?	*Are there any dogs?* *Is there a dog?*
M<u>e</u>ron.	*Yes, there is/are.*
Wala'.	*No, there aren't any.*

May <u>a</u>so ba si Alfred?	*Does Alfred have any dogs?* *Does Alfred have a dog?*
M<u>e</u>ron.	*Yes, he has one/some.*
Wala'.	*No, he doesn't have any.*

M<u>e</u>ron ba?	*Are there any?*
Mar<u>a</u>mi ba?	*Are there many?*
Wala' ba?	*Isn't there any?* *Is there none?*

<u>M</u>eron/mar<u>a</u>mi/wala' + nito etc.

M<u>e</u>ron nito.	*There are some of these.*
Mar<u>a</u>mi nito.	*There are many of these.*
Wala' nito.	*There are none of these.*

M<u>e</u>ron niyan si Alfred.	*Alfred has some of those. (near you)*
Mar<u>a</u>mi niyan si Alfred.	*Alfred has many of those. (near you)*
Wala' niyan si Alfred.	*Alfred has none of those. (near you)*

See also: Ng demonstrative pronouns (p. 59), Clarification: near me etc. (p. 56)

May/<u>me</u>ron/ma<u>ra</u>mi/wala' + verb/adjective/etc. used as a noun

Indicating existence or non-existence

May maganda. <u>Me</u>rong maganda.	*There's someone (who's) pretty.* *There's something (that's) pretty.* *There's somewhere (that's) pretty.*
May <u>na</u>sa labas. <u>Me</u>rong <u>na</u>sa labas.	*There's someone (who's) outside.* *There's something (that's) outside.* *There's somewhere (that's) outside (e.g.* *outside the city).*

May ku<u>ma</u>in. <u>Me</u>rong ku<u>ma</u>in.	*Someone ate.* Lit. *There's someone who ate.**
Ma<u>ra</u>ming ku<u>ma</u>in.	*Many people ate.* Lit. *There were many that ate.*
Walang ku<u>ma</u>in.	*Nobody ate.* Lit. *There were none that ate.*

* **May** *(there's some)* **ku<u>ma</u>in** *(one who ate).*

See also: Verbs, adjectives etc. used as nouns (p. 101)

Indicating possession or non-possession

May maganda si Fred. <u>Me</u>rong maganda si Fred.	*Fred has something (that's)* *pretty.*

May ki<u>na</u>in si Fred. <u>Me</u>rong ki<u>na</u>in si Fred.	*Fred ate something.* Lit. *Fred had something eaten.**
Ma<u>ra</u>ming ki<u>na</u>in si Fred.	*Fred ate a lot.* Lit. *Fred had a lot of things eaten.*
Walang ki<u>na</u>in si Fred.	*Fred ate nothing.* *Fred didn't eat anything.* Lit. *Fred had nothing eaten.*

* **May** *(had some)* **ki<u>na</u>in** *(thing eaten)* **si Fred.**

May pinuntahan si Fred. <u>Me</u>rong pinuntahan si Fred.	*Fred went somewhere.* Lit. *Fred had some place gone to.*
Ma<u>ra</u>ming pinuntahan si Fred.	*Fred went to many places.* Lit. *Fred had many places gone to.*
Walang pinuntahan si Fred.	*Fred went nowhere.* *Fred didn't go anywhere.* Lit. *Fred had no place gone to.*

May ginawa' si Fred. <u>Me</u>rong ginawa' si Fred.	*Fred did something.* Lit. *Fred had something done.*
May gi<u>na</u>gawa' si Fred. <u>Me</u>rong gi<u>na</u>gawa' si Fred.	*Fred is doing something.* Lit. *Fred has something being done.*
May <u>ga</u>gawin si Fred. <u>Me</u>rong <u>ga</u>gawin si Fred.	*Fred is going to do something.* Also: *Fred has something to do.* Lit. *Fred has something that will be done / to be done.*

Maraming gagawin si Fred.	*Fred is going to do a lot of things.* Also: *Fred has a lot of things to do.* Lit. *Fred has a lot of things that will be done / to be done.*
Walang gagawin si Fred.	*Fred isn't going to do anything.* Also: *Fred has nothing to do.* Lit. *Fred has nothing that will be done / to be done.*

See also: Verbs, adjectives etc. used as nouns (p. 101)

May/meron/marami/wala' + noun + verb

The noun and the verb are linked up by **na/-ng**.

May babaeng dumating. **Merong babaeng dumating.** **May dumating na babae.** **Merong dumating na babae.**	*A woman came.* Lit. *There's a woman who came.* / *There's someone who came who's a woman.*
Maraming babaeng dumating. **Maraming dumating na babae.**	*Many women came.*
Walang babaeng dumating. **Walang dumating na babae.**	*No women came.*

May project *na* gagawin si Fred. May gagawing project si Fred.	*Fred is going to do a project.* Also: *Fred has a project to do.* Lit. *Fred has a project that will be done. / Fred has something that will be done that is a project.*

See also:

- **Na/-ng** (p. 34)
- **May/meron/marami/wala'** + verb/adjective/etc. used as a noun (p. 383)

Walang ka- +rep2

walang ka- +rep2

there is/are/was/were no... at all,
has/have/had no... at all

Walang kakotse-kotse.	*There are no cars at all.*
Walang kapera-pera si John.	*John has no money at all.*

See also: Syllable repetition (p. 33)

Questions

Yes/no questions

A statement can be turned into a yes/no question by raising the pitch at the end. **Ba** may also be used.

Belgian si Paul.	*Paul is Belgian.*
Belgian (ba) si Paul?	*Is Paul Belgian?*

May aso.	*There's a dog.*
May aso (ba)?	*Are there any dogs?* *Is there a dog?*

See also: **Ba** (p. 369)

Answering affirmative yes/no questions

Belgian ba si Paul?	*Is Paul Belgian?*
Oo, Belgian siya.	*Yes, he's Belgian.*
Hindi', hindi' siya Belgian.	*No, he isn't Belgian.*

Sasama ka ba?	Are you coming along?
Oo, sasama ako.	Yes, I'm coming along.
Hindi', hindi' ako sasama.	No, I'm not coming along.

Answering negative yes/no questions

Hindi' ba Belgian si Paul?	Isn't Paul Belgian?
Belgian.	Yes, he's Belgian.
Hindi', hindi' siya Belgian.	No, he isn't Belgian.

Hindi' ka ba sasama?	Aren't you coming along?
Sasama.	Yes, I'm coming along.
Hindi', hindi' ako sasama.	No, I'm not coming along.

Answering yes/no questions starting with may, meron or wala'

May aso ba?	Are there any dogs? Is there a dog?
Meron.*	Yes, there is/are.
Wala'.	No, there aren't any.

May <u>a</u>so ba si Alfred?	*Does Alfred have any dogs?* *Does Alfred have a dog?*
<u>Me</u>ron.*	*Yes, he has one/some.*
Wala'.	*No, he doesn't have any.*

* Yes/no questions starting with **may** or **<u>me</u>ron** can also be answered with **<u>o</u>o** *(yes)*.

See also: **May, mayroon/<u>me</u>ron, ma<u>ra</u>mi, wala'** (p. 379)

Confirmation questions

Di ba and **ano ('no)** are used in questions asking to confirm something.

1. **di ba** – may be used at the beginning or at the end of a sentence.

Na<u>tu</u>log ka, di ba? Di ba na<u>tu</u>log ka?	*You slept, didn't you?* *Didn't you sleep?*
Ang ganda, di ba? Di ba ang ganda?	*It's so pretty, isn't it?* *Isn't it so pretty?*

See also: **Ba** (p. 369)

2. **'no** – can only be used at the end of a sentence.

Ang ganda 'no?	*It's so pretty, isn't it?*

'no can also be used with a falling intonation to express certainty or confidence.

Natulog ka 'no.	*You slept, didn't you.* *(I'm sure you did.)*

Answering affirmative confirmation questions

Belgian si Paul, di ba? Di ba Belgian si Paul?	*Paul is Belgian, isn't he?* *Isn't Paul Belgian?*
Oo, Belgian siya.	*Yes, he's Belgian.*
Hindi', hindi' siya Belgian.	*No, he isn't Belgian.*

Sasama ka, di ba? Di ba sasama ka?	*You're coming along, aren't you?* *Aren't you coming along?*
Oo, sasama ako.	*Yes, I'm coming along.*
Hindi', hindi' ako sasama.	*No, I'm not coming along.*

Answering negative confirmation questions

Hindi' Belgian si Paul, di ba?	*Paul isn't Belgian, is he?*
Oo, hindi' siya Belgian.	*That's right, he isn't Belgian.*
Hindi', Belgian siya.	*That's not right, he's Belgian.*

Hindi' ka <u>sasa</u>ma, di ba?	*You're not coming along, are you?*
<u>Oo</u>, hindi' ako <u>sasa</u>ma.	*That's right, I'm not coming along.*
Hindi', <u>sasa</u>ma ako.	*That's not right, I'm coming along.*

Alternative questions

O *("or")* is used in questions presenting two or more choices.

Belgian ba si Paul, o Ameri<u>ka</u>no?	*Is Paul Belgian or American?*
<u>Sasa</u>ma ka ba o hindi'?	*Are you coming along or not?*
<u>Ka</u>kanta ka ba o <u>sasa</u>yaw?	*Will you sing or dance?*

Answering alternative questions

Belgian ba si Paul, o Ameri<u>ka</u>no?	*Is Paul Belgian or American?*
Belgian.	*Belgian.*
Ameri<u>ka</u>no.	*American.*

Please-repeat questions

The following expressions can be used to ask someone to repeat what he or she has just said.

Ano po'?	*Pardon me? Sorry?* (polite)
Ano?	*What? Sorry?*
Ha?	*Huh?*

Ano pong sinabi niyo? **Ano pong sabi niyo?**	*What did you say?* (polite)
Anong sinabi mo? **Anong sabi mo?** **Ano kamo?**	*What did you say?*

Sino sabi mo ang darating? **Sino kamo ang darating?**	*Who did you say was coming?*
Ano sabi mo ang dahilan? **Ano kamo ang dahilan?**	*What did you say was the reason?*

See also: **Po'/Ho'** (p. 369)

Questions using question words

Overview of question words

The following question words are used in Tagalog. The plural forms may
be used when a plural answer is expected.

singular or plural	plural	meaning
ano	anu-ano	*what*
alin	alin-alin	*which*
kailan (<u>ke</u>lan)	ka<u>i</u>-kailan	*when*
<u>ba</u>kit	-	*why*
<u>si</u>no	<u>si</u>nu-<u>si</u>no	*who(m), which (person/s)*
<u>ni</u>no	<u>ni</u>nu-<u>ni</u>no	*whose, who(m)*
ka<u>ni</u>no	ka<u>ni</u>-ka<u>ni</u>no	*whose, who(m)*
<u>na</u> ka<u>ni</u>no	<u>na</u> ka<u>ni</u>-ka<u>ni</u>no	*with whom (in whose possession, at whose place/s)*
saan (san)	saan-saan	*where, which (place/s), what*
<u>na</u>saan (<u>na</u>san, <u>a</u>san)	-	*where (is/are/was/were), which (place/s) (is/are/was/were)*

pa**a**no (**pa**no)	paa-pa**a**no	*how* (manner, means)
kumusta / kamusta (musta)	-	*how (is/are/was/were)* (quality, condition)
ga**a**no (**ga**no)	ga**a**-ga**a**no	*how* (extent, degree, quantity)
ilan	ilan-ilan	*how many*
mag**ka**no	mag**ka**-mag**ka**no	*how much* (price)

Ba may be used in questions using question words.

Saan (ba) pumunta si Fred?	*Where did Fred go?*

See also: **Ba** (p. 369)

Using question words

Ano

what

Ano iyon?	*What's that?*
Ano ang kina**in mo?**	*What did you eat?*
Ano ang nangya**ri?**	*What happened?*

Ano -ng

Anong <u>kla</u>se?	*What kind?*
Anong <u>kla</u>seng pag<u>ka</u>in?	*What kind of food?*
Anong <u>o</u>ras?	*What time?*
Anong <u>o</u>ras <u>da</u>rating si Fred?	*What time will Fred arrive?*

See also: **Na/-ng** (p. 34)

A: **Bumili siya ng mater<u>ya</u>les <u>pa</u>ra sa project.** B: <u>**Pa**</u>**ra sa ano?**	A: *He/she bought materials for the project.* B: *What for?* Lit. *For what?*
A: <u>**Na**</u>**sa drawer ang bag.** B: <u>**Na**</u>**sa ano ang bag?**	A: *The bag is in the drawer.* B: *What is the bag in?* Lit. *The bag is in what?*
A: **Mata<u>li</u>no siya.** B: **Maano siya?**	A: *He/she's smart.* B: *What is he/she like?* Lit. *He/she's like what?*
A: <u>**Na**</u>**pakata<u>li</u>no niya.** B: <u>**Na**</u>**pakaano niya?**	A: *He/she's very smart.* B: *What is he/she very much like?* Lit. *He/she's very much like what?*

A: **Nag-jogging ako.**	A: *I went jogging.*
B: **Nag-ano ka?**	B: *What did you do?*
	Lit. *You did what?*
A: **Na<u>hu</u>log ako.**	A: *I fell.*
B: **Naano ka?**	B: *What happened to you?*
	Lit. *You experienced what?*

Ano (or **kuwan**) can also be used to say *thingy, whatsisname* or *whatsername.*

Na<u>hu</u>log ang ano.	*The thingy fell.*
Na<u>hu</u>log ang kuwan.	
Tu<u>ma</u>wag si ano.	*Whatsisname called.*
Tu<u>ma</u>wag si kuwan.	

Note: **Ano ang** may sometimes be shortened to **anong.**

Ano ang pa<u>nga</u>lan mo?	*What's your name?*
Anong pa<u>nga</u>lan mo?	

Alin

which

Alin ang <u>ba</u>hay?	*Which (one) is the house?*
Alin sa mga <u>ba</u>hay?	*Which of the houses?*

Alin -ng

Aling bahay?	*Which house?*
Nasa aling bayan?	*In which town?* *Which town is it in?*

See also: **Na/-ng** (p. 34)

Note: **Sino**, instead of **alin**, is generally used to ask about persons.

Sinong teacher?	*Which teacher?*
Sinu-sinong teacher?	*Which teachers?*

Kailan (kelan)

when

Kailan babalik si John?	*When will John come back?*
Kailan ang birthday mo?	*When is your birthday?*
Mula' kailan?	*From when?*
Mula' pa kailan? Kailan pa?	*Since when?*
Hanggang kailan?	*Till when?*

Bakit

why

Bakit siya umalis?	*Why did he/she leave?*
Bakit ginawa' ni John iyon?	*Why did John do that?*
Bakit itim?	*Why black?*

Sino

who(m), which (person/s)

Sino ang kumain dito?	*Who ate here?*
Sino siya?	*Who is he/she?*
Sino sa mga bata'?	*Which of the children?*

Sino -ng

Sinong teacher?	*Which teacher?*

See also: **Na/-ng** (p. 34)

Note: **Sino ang** may sometimes be shortened to **sinong**.

Sino ang nanalo? **Sinong nanalo?**	*Who won?*

Nino

whose, who(m)

Nino is used in the same way as a Ng phrase referring to a person.

A: **Bag ni Mary ito.**	A: *This is Mary's bag.*
B: **Bag nino ito?**	B: *Whose bag is this?*
A: **Kinain ni Fred ang mangga.**	A: *Fred ate the mango.*
B: **Kinain nino ang mangga?**	B: *Who ate the mango?*
A: **Nasa tabi ng teacher si John.**	A: *John is (sitting/standing) next to the teacher.*
B: **Nasa tabi nino si John?**	B: *Who is John (sitting/standing) next to?*
	Lit. *John is beside whom?*

See also: Ng phrase (p. 70)

Kanino

whose, who(m)

Kanino is used in the same way as a Sa phrase referring to a person.

A: **Kay Mary ito.**	A: *This is Mary's.*
B: **Kanino ito?**	B: *Whose is this?*
A: **Tumawag kay John si Fred.**	A: *Fred called John.*
B: **Tumawag kanino si Fred?**	B: *Who did Fred call?*
Kanino tumawag si Fred?	Lit. *Fred called whom?*
A: **Para kay Fred ito.**	A: *This is for Fred.*
B: **Para kanino ito?**	B: *Who is this for?*
	Lit. *This is for whom?*

Ka<u>ni</u>no -ng – *whose*

Ka<u>ni</u>nong bag ito?	*Whose bag is this?*

See also: Sa phrase (p. 70), **Na/-ng** (p. 34)

<u>Na</u> ka<u>ni</u>no

with whom (in whose possession, at whose place/s)

<u>Na</u> ka<u>ni</u>no is used in the same way as a Nasa phrase referring to a person.

A: <u>Na</u> kay Fred ang libro.	A: *Fred has the book.*
B: <u>Na</u> ka<u>ni</u>no ang libro?	Lit. *The book is with Fred.*
	B: *Who has the book?*
	Lit. *The book is with whom?*
A: <u>Na</u> kina <u>Lo</u>la si John.	A: *John is at Lola's.*
B: <u>Na</u> ka<u>ni</u>no si John?	B: *Where (at whose place) is John?*

See also: <u>Na</u>sa (p. 289)

Saan (san)

where, which (place/s), what

Saan is used in the same way as a Sa phrase that doesn't refer to a person.

Saan ka ku<u>main</u>?	*Where did you eat?*
Saan ka <u>pu</u>punta?	*Where are you going?*
Saan ang party?	*Where is the party?*
<u>Ga</u>ling saan ito?**	*Where is this from?* Lit. *This is from where?*
Taga-saan siya?	*Where is he/she from?* Lit. *He/she is from where?*
<u>Pa</u>ra saan?**	*What for?*

Saan -ng

Saang school ka pu<u>ma</u>pa<u>s</u>ok?	*Which school do you go to?*

See also: Sa phrase (p. 70), **Na/-ng** (p. 34)

Nasaan (nasan, asan)

where (is/are/was/were), which (place/s) (is/are/was/were)

Nasaan is used in the same way as a Nasa phrase that doesn't refer to a person.

A: **Nasa drawer ang bag.**	A: *The bag is in the drawer.*
B: **Nasaan ang bag?**	B: *Where is the bag?*
A: **Nasa school si Fred.**	A: *Fred is in school.*
B: **Nasaan si Fred?**	B: *Where is Fred?*

Nasaan -ng

A: **Nasa Quezon City ako.**	A: *I'm in Quezon City.*
B: **Nasaang siyudad ka?**	B: *Which city are you in?*
	Lit. *You are in which city?*

Alternative: **saan nandoon (san nandon)**

San nandon ang bag?	*Where is the bag?*

See also: **Nasa** (p. 289), **Na/-ng** (p. 34)

Paano (pano)

how (manner, means)

Paano ka magtrabaho?	*How do you work?*
Paano ka nagtrabaho?	*How did you work?*

Paano pumunta si Mary sa Maynila'?	*How did Mary go to Manila?*
Paano nangyari iyon?	*How did that happen?*

Also:

Paano kung...	*What if...*
Paano kung manalo ka?	*What if you win?*

Kumusta / kamusta (musta)

how (is/are/was/were) (quality, condition)

Kumusta ang byahe?	*How is/was the trip?*
Kumusta ang buhay sa Maynila'?	*How's life in Manila?*
Kumusta? (greeting)	*How are you?*

Gaano (gano)

how (extent, degree, quantity)

gaano ka- + adjective root
how big, fast etc.

Gaano kalaki ang bahay?	*How big is the house?*
Gaano kabilis tumakbo si Fred?	*How fast does Fred run?* *How fast did Fred run?*

| Gaano kadalas magluto' si John? | How often does John cook? |
| Gaano karami? | How much? How many? |

Plural: **gaano ka-** +rep1 + adjective root

| Gaano kalaki ang mga bahay? Gaano kalalaki ang mga bahay? | How big are the houses? |

Note: Using the plural form is optional.

See also: Syllable repetition (p. 33)

Ilan

how many

| Ilan ang payong sa kotse? | How many umbrellas are in the car? Lit. How many are the umbrellas in the car? |

Ilan -ng

| Ilang payong ang nasa kotse? | How many umbrellas are in the car? |
| Ilang beses kumain si John? | How many times did John eat? |

Ilang taon na siya?	How old is he/she? Lit. How many years now is he/she?

See also: **Na/-ng** (p. 34)

Magkano

how much (price)

Magkano ang ballpen?	How much is the pen?
Magkano ang mangga?	How much are the mangoes? How much is the mango?

magkakano – *how much each*

Magkakano ang mangga?	How much are the mangoes each?

Other sentence structures

Negation

Hindi'

hindi'

not, n't

Hindi' Belgian si Mark.	*Mark isn't Belgian.*
Hindi' mayaman si Mark.	*Mark isn't rich.*
Hindi' nagluto' si Mark.	*Mark didn't cook.*
Hindi' nagluluto' si Mark.	*Mark doesn't cook.*
Hindi' magluluto' si Mark.	*Mark won't cook.*

Hindi' may also be followed by the basic form of verbs expressing ability, i.e. certain ma- (p. 136), maka-, makapag-, makapang- (p. 166) and mapa- (p. 180) verbs.

Hindi' nakakalakad si John. Hindi' makalakad si John.	John can't walk.
Nakakalakad si John.	John can walk.

hinding hindi'

not at all, certainly not

Hinding hindi' siya bakla'.	He's not gay at all.

hindi'... kahit kailan

never

Hindi' nagtrabaho si Mark kahit kailan.	Mark never worked.
Hindi' magtatrabaho si Mark kahit kailan.	Mark will never work.

Ewan

ewan + Ng phrase

not known

Ewan (ko).	_I don't know._ Lit. _Not known by me._
Ewan namin.	_We (excl. you) don't know._
Ewan natin.	_We (incl. you) don't know._
Ewan raw niya.	_He/she/they said he/she didn't know._
Ewan raw nila.	_He/she/they said they didn't know._

See also: Ng phrase (p. 70)

ewan... kung [1]

not known if/whether

Ewan ko kung aalis siya.	_I don't know if he/she's leaving._

ewan... kung [2]

not known who/what/etc.

Ewan ko kung <u>si</u>no.	*I don't know who.*
Ewan ko kung <u>ba</u>kit.	*I don't know why.*

See also: Overview of question words (p. 393), Using question words (p. 394)

Ni

ni + hindi'/wala'/etc.

not even

<u>Ni</u> <u>la</u>pis, hindi' siya nagdala.	*He/she didn't even bring a pencil.* Lit. *Even a pencil, he/she didn't bring.*
<u>Ni</u> <u>la</u>pis, wala' ako.	*I don't even have a pencil.* Lit. *Even a pencil, I don't have.*
<u>Ni</u> teacher, hindi' dumating.	*Not even a teacher came.* Lit. *Even a teacher, didn't come.*
<u>Ni</u> ang teacher, hindi' dumating.	*Not even the teacher came.* Lit. *Even the teacher, didn't come.*

_Ni... ni_

ni... ni + hindi'/wala'/etc.
neither... nor

Ni pagka̱in **ni** tu̱big, wala' sila.	_They have neither food nor water._ Lit. _Either food or water, they don't have._
Ni si Fred **ni** si John, hindi' dumating.	_Neither Fred nor John came._ Lit. _Either Fred or John, didn't come._

Other

wala'
- May, mayroon/me̱ron, mara̱mi, wala' (p. 379)
- Wala' sa, wala' ri̱to (p. 294)

huwag
- Huwag (p. 225)

a̱yaw
- Pseudo-verbs (p. 236)

Kahit (na) ano etc.

"Kahit (na) / maski (na) + question word" is understood as follows:

kahit (na) ano	*anything, whatever, no matter what*
kahit (na) alin	*any, whichever, no matter which*
kahit (na) kailan	*anytime, whenever, no matter when*

kahit (na) sino	*anybody, whoever, no matter who* *any (person), whichever (person), no matter which (person)*
kahit (na) kanino	*anybody, whoever, no matter who*
kahit (na) na kanino	*with whomever, no matter with whom*

kahit (na) saan	*anywhere, wherever, no matter where* *any (place), whichever (place), no matter which (place)*
kahit (na) nasaan	*anywhere, wherever, no matter where* *any (place), whichever (place), no matter which (place) (is/are/was/were)*

kahit (na) paano	*however (in whatever way), no matter how (something happens etc.)*
kahit (na) gaano	*however (much/good/big/etc.), no matter how (much/good/big/etc.)*

<u>ka</u>hit (na) ilan	*however many, no matter how many*
<u>ka</u>hit (na) mag<u>ka</u>no	*however much (something costs), no matter how much (something costs)*

Sentences:

<u>Ka</u>hit ano, <u>ga</u>gawin ko.	*Whatever it is, I'll do it. / I'll do anything.*
<u>Ka</u>hit na ano ang gusto mo, i<u>bi</u>bigay ko.	*Whatever you want, I'll give it to you.*
<u>Ka</u>hit na ano ang mang<u>ya</u>ri, hindi' kita <u>ii</u>wan.	*Whatever happens, I won't leave you.*
<u>Ka</u>hit mag<u>ka</u>no, <u>bi</u>bilhin ko.	*No matter how much it costs, I'll buy it.*
Huwag kang <u>pu</u>punta <u>ka</u>hit saan.	*Don't go anywhere.*

Note:

<u>ka</u>hit (na) pa<u>a</u>no	*however (in whatever way), no matter how*
<u>ka</u>hit (na) *pa*pa<u>a</u>no	*somehow, one way or another*

An alternative, more formal way of saying <u>ka</u>hit (na) ano/alin/etc. is anu<u>man</u>, alin<u>man</u>, kailan<u>man</u>, <u>si</u>numan, ka<u>ni</u>numan, saan<u>man</u>, ilan<u>man</u>. However, they are not always interchangeable.

See also: Overview of question words (p. 393), Using question words (p. 394)

At, o, pero etc.

at

and

Tu<u>ma</u>wag si Mary at si John.	*Mary and John called.*
<u>Ka</u>kanta at <u>sa</u>sayaw si John.	*John will sing and dance.*

At may be shortened to **'t** if the preceding word ends in a vowel or /n/ (**'t** replaces /n/).

maganda at mata<u>li</u>no **maganda't mata<u>li</u>no**	*pretty and smart*
ma<u>ya</u>man at mata<u>li</u>no **ma<u>ya</u>ma't mata<u>li</u>no**	*rich and smart*

at saka (tsaka, chaka)

and... too; and also

Tu<u>ma</u>wag si Mary, at saka si John.	*Mary called, and John too.*
Maganda siya, at saka mata<u>li</u>no.	*She's pretty, and smart too.*

(at) pati

and... too; as well

Tumawag si Mary, at pati si John.	*Mary called, and John too.*
Pati si John, tumawag.	*John called as well.*

o

or

itim o puti'	*black or white*
Sabado ba ngayon o Linggo?	*Is it Saturday today or Sunday?*

o kaya'

or (else)

itim o kaya' puti'	*black or white*
bukas, o kaya' sa Lunes	*tomorrow, or else on Monday*

pero

but

Mayaman siya pero kuripot.	*He/she's rich but stingy.*
Gusto kong mag-shopping pero wala' akong pera.	*I want to go shopping but I don't have any money.*

kundi'

but (rather)

Hindi' si John ang dumating, kundi' si Fred.	*It wasn't John who came, but Fred.*
Hindi' Ameri<u>ka</u>no si John, kundi' Canadian.	*John is not American, but Canadian.*

Hindi' lang... kundi'

not only... but (also)

Hindi' lang pag<u>ka</u>in, kundi' damit.	*Not only food, but also clothing.*

Wala'... kundi'

no one/nothing... but (except for)

Walang dumating kundi' si John.	*No one came but John.*

Buti at, salamat at etc.

At can be used to explain why something is good/bad/etc. or why someone feels happy/sad/etc.

buti at, mabuti at *it's good (that)*	Mabuti at nandito ka.	*It's good (that) you're here.*
buti na lang (at), mabuti na lang (at) *good thing, thank goodness*	Buti na lang (at) nandito ka.	*Good thing you're here.*
salamat at *thank goodness*	Salamat at nandito ka.	*Thank goodness you're here.*

swerte at *it's pure luck that*	Swerte at nandito ka.	*It's pure luck that you're here.*
milagro at *it's a miracle that*	Milagro at nandito ka.	*It's a miracle that you're here.*
malas at *it's unfortunate that*	Malas at wala' ka rito.	*It's unfortunate that you're not here.*
sayang (at) *too bad, it's a pity*	Sayang (at) wala' ka rito.	*Too bad you're not here.*

magulat at *to be surprised that*	Nagulat ako at nandito sila.	*I'm/I was surprised that they're here.*
masaya at *happy that*	Masaya ako at nandito ka.	*I'm happy that you're here.*

Indirect speech or thought

Introduced by na/-ng or kung

Na/-ng and kung can be used to introduce what someone says, thinks etc.

na/-ng

that

Sinabi ko kay Mary *na* nandito si John.	*I told Mary (that) John was here.*
Sinabi ko *na* nandito si John.	*I said (that) John was here.*
Alam ko*ng* nandito si John.	*I know (that) John is/was here.*
Naalala ko*ng* nandito si John.	*I remembered that John was here.*

kung [1]

if, whether

Tinanong ko si/kay Mary *kung* nandito si John.	*I asked Mary whether John was here.*
Tinanong ko *kung* nandito si John.	*I asked whether John was here.*
Alam ko *kung* nandito si John.	*I know whether John is/was here.*
Hindi' ko maalala *kung* nandito si John.	*I can't remember whether John was here.*

kung ²

used before question words

Si<u>na</u>bi ko *kung* <u>ba</u>kit.	*I said why.*
Tinanong ko *kung* <u>ba</u>kit.	*I asked why.*
Tinanong ko *kung* kailan <u>ba</u>balik si John.	*I asked when John would come back.*
Alam ko *kung* <u>ba</u>kit.	*I know why.*
Alam mo ba *kung* <u>ba</u>kit?	*Do you know why?*
Naa<u>la</u>la ko *kung* <u>ba</u>kit.	*I remembered why.*

See also: **Na/-ng** (p. 34), Overview of question words (p. 393), Using question words (p. 394)

Not introduced by na/-ng or kung

(Ang) <u>sa</u>bi ko, nan<u>di</u>to si John.	*I said John was here.*
<u>Sa</u>bi ko kay Mary, nan<u>di</u>to si John.	*I told Mary John was here.*
<u>Sa</u>bi niya, nan<u>di</u>to (raw) si John.	*He/she said John was here.*
<u>Sa</u>bi ko, <u>ba</u>kit?	*I said, why?*
Nan<u>di</u>to siya <u>ka</u>ko. Nan<u>di</u>to <u>ka</u>ko siya.	*I said, he/she's here.*

Sa tingin ko, umalis na si John.	*I think John has left.*
Sa tingin mo ba, umalis na si John?	*Do you think John has left?*
Palagay ko, umalis na si John.	*I think (in my opinion) John has left.*
Pakiramdam ko, umalis na si John.	*I have a feeling John has left.*

Ang pag<u>ka</u>intindi ko, umalis na si John.	*My understanding is John has left.*
Ang alam ko, umalis na si John.	*What I know is that John has left.*
A<u>ka</u>la' ko (ba), umalis na si John.*	*I thought (mistakenly) John had left.*

(Ang) <u>i</u>big kong sa<u>bi</u>hin, umalis na si John.	*I mean, John has left.*
(Ang) <u>i</u>big mong sa<u>bi</u>hin, umalis na si John.	*You mean, John has left.*

Ba<u>li</u>ta' ko, umalis na si John. Ang rinig ko, umalis na si John.	*I've heard John has left.*

* See also: **Ba** (p. 369)

See also: Verbs expressing mental states or perception (p. 228)

Sentences with no POD

The following sentences have no POD (p. 35):

1. yes, no, maybe

Oo.	*Yes.*
Siguro.	*Maybe.*

2. some greetings and other social expressions (p. 427)

Kumusta?	*How are you?*

3. some interjections (p. 438)

Aray!	*Ouch!*

4. sentences with a verb in recently completed form (p. 215)

Kararating lang ni Mary.	*Mary has just arrived.*

5. some commands and requests (p. 220)

Takbo!	*Run!*
Pakibuhat ng bag.	*Could you carry the bag.*

6. some sentences with a pseudo-verb (p. 236)

Gusto ni John ng mangga.	*John wants a mango.*
Gustong kumain ni John.	*John wants to eat.*

7. sentences with an adjective intensified by a Group 2 intensifier (p. 259)

Napakalaki ng aso!	*The dog is so big!*

8. some **may, mayroon/meron, marami** and **wala'** sentences (p. 379)

May aso.	*There's a dog.*
Maraming aso.	*There are many dogs.*

9. some sentences with a **magka-** verb (p. 155) or **magkaroon** (p. 156)

Nagkagulo. **Nagkaroon ng gulo.**	*A commotion broke out.* *Chaos broke out.*
Nagkaproblema. **Nagkaroon ng problema.**	*A problem occurred.*

10. sentences expressing time

Alas dos na.	*It's two o'clock.*
Tanghali' na.	*It's noon.*
Maaga pa.	*It's still early.*

Magde-December na.*	*It will soon be December.*
Pasko na!	*It's Christmas!*

* See also: **mag-** [5] (p. 149)

11. sentences expressing natural phenomena

Umuulan.*	*It's raining.*
Bumaha' kahapon.	*It flooded yesterday.*
Lumilindol!	*There's an earthquake!* Lit. *It's "earthquaking!"*
Kumukulog at kumikidlat.	*There's thunder and lightning.*
Mainit sa Maynila'.	*It's hot in Manila.*

* See also: **(-)um-** [2] (p. 203)

POD-first sentences

In POD-first sentences, the POD (p. 35) comes before the News (p. 35). The POD is followed by either **ay** or a pause.

POD–ay–News

This sentence pattern is generally used in written Tagalog and formal spoken Tagalog.

Ang bata' ay kumain. **(Kumain ang bata'.)**	*The child ate.*
Ikaw ay maganda. **(Maganda ka.)**	*You are pretty.*
Ikaw ay nakita' ko. **(Nakita' kita.)**	*I saw you.* Lit. *You were seen by me.*

Ay may be shortened to **'y** if the preceding word ends in a vowel, /n/ or /w/ (**'y** replaces /n/ or /w/).

Siya ay maganda. **Siya'y maganda.**	*She's pretty.*
Ikaw ay maganda. **Ika'y maganda.**	*You're pretty.*

See also: **Ikaw** and **ka** (p. 54), **Kita** (p. 71)

POD–pause–News

This sentence pattern may be used when showing contrast.

Si John, <u>na</u>sa May<u>ni</u>la'. Si Mary, <u>na</u>sa Cebu.	*John is in Manila, while Mary is in Cebu.*
Ang <u>pu</u>sa', ku<u>ma</u>in. Ang <u>a</u>so, hindi'.	*The cat ate but the dog didn't.*

Additional notes on word order

1. A Sa phrase (p. 70) indicating location or direction may be placed at the beginning of a sentence for emphasis or to show contrast.

Ku<u>ma</u>in *sa school* ang ba<u>ba</u>e. Ku<u>ma</u>in ang ba<u>ba</u>e *sa school*.	*The woman ate at school.*
Sa school ku<u>ma</u>in ang ba<u>ba</u>e.	*The woman ate at school.* *It's at school that the woman ate.*
Sa school ku<u>ma</u>in ang ba<u>ba</u>e. Sa <u>ba</u>hay naman ku<u>ma</u>in ang la<u>la</u>ki.	*The woman ate at school, while the man ate at home.*

Sumulat *kay Mary* ang ba<u>bae</u>. Sumulat ang ba<u>bae</u> *kay Mary*.	*The woman wrote (to) Mary.*
Kay Mary su<u>mu</u>lat ang ba<u>bae</u>.	*The woman wrote (to) Mary.* *It's Mary that the woman wrote* *(to).*
Kay Mary su<u>mu</u>lat ang ba<u>bae</u>. Kay John naman su<u>mu</u>lat ang la<u>la</u>ki.	*The woman wrote (to) Mary,* *while the man wrote (to) John.*

2. Describing words expressing time or location may be placed at the beginning of a sentence for emphasis or to show contrast.

Nag-<u>a</u>ral si Mary *<u>di</u>to*. Nag-<u>a</u>ral *<u>di</u>to* si Mary.	*Mary studied here.*
<u>Di</u>to nag-<u>a</u>ral si Mary.	*Mary studied here.* *It's here that Mary studied.*
<u>Di</u>to nag-<u>a</u>ral si Mary. Doon naman nag-<u>a</u>ral si John.	*Mary studied here, while John* *studied there.*

<u>A</u>alis si John *<u>bu</u>kas*. <u>A</u>alis *<u>bu</u>kas* si John.	*John is leaving tomorrow.*
<u>Bu</u>kas <u>a</u>alis si John.	*John is leaving tomorrow.* *It's tomorrow that John will* *leave.*
<u>Bu</u>kas <u>a</u>alis si John. Hindi' ngayon.	*John is leaving tomorrow, not* *today.*

See also: Expressing location (p. 289), Expressing time, frequency or duration (p. 300)

Greetings and other social expressions

For different times of day

Magandang umaga.	*Good morning.*
Magandang umaga rin.	*Good morning.* Lit. *Good morning too.*

Magandang tanghali'.	Lit. *Good noon.*
Magandang hapon.	*Good afternoon.*
Magandang gabi.	*Good evening.*

See also: Parts of the day (p. 301)

How are you?

Kumusta? Kumusta ka na?	*How are you? / How's it going?*
Mabuti (naman). Ikaw, kumusta? OK lang. Ikaw, kumusta?	*Fine. / I'm good. How about you?*

For chance meetings

San ang punta mo? San ang lakad mo?	*Where are you going?*
San ka galing?	*Where are you coming from?*
Dyan lang.	*Just there. / Just around the corner. (Nowhere in particular.)*
Sa mall. May bibilhin lang.	*I'm just going to the mall to buy something.*

When someone is eating

Kain tayo!	Lit. *Let's eat!* (often used as a greeting by someone who's eating)
Sige, salamat.	*No, thanks.* Lit. *OK, thanks.*

At someone's home

Tao po'.	*Anyone home?* Lit. *(There's a) person.*
Tuloy. Tuloy ka.	*Come in.*
Upo' ka. Maupo' ka.	*Have a seat.*

On the phone

Hello, <u>pwe</u>de pong maka<u>u</u>sap si John.	*Hello, I'd like to speak to John, please.*
Hello, nandyan po' ba si John?	*Hello, is John in/there?*
Bye.	*Bye.*

Bye

Mau<u>u</u>na na ako. <u>A</u>alis na ako. <u>La</u>lakad na ako. <u>Tu</u>tuloy na ako.	*I'll leave now. / Gotta go.*
<u>U</u>uwi' na ako.	*I'll go home now.*
<u>I</u>ngat.	*Take care.*

Special occasions

Mali<u>ga</u>yang Pasko.	*Merry Christmas.*
Ma<u>ni</u>gong <u>Ba</u>gong Taon.	*Happy New Year.*
Mali<u>ga</u>yang Kaarawan. Mali<u>ga</u>yang <u>Ba</u>ti'.	*Happy Birthday.*

Thanks

Sa<u>la</u>mat.	*Thanks.*
Ma<u>ra</u>ming sa<u>la</u>mat.	*Thanks a lot. / Thank you very much.*
Wala' 'yon. (informal) Walang anuman. (formal)	*You're welcome. / No problem.*

Other

Sandali' lang.	*Just a minute.*
<u>Te</u>ka lang. <u>Te</u>ka <u>mu</u>na.	*Wait a minute.*
Ma<u>ki</u>kiraan po'.	*Excuse me.* (used when passing in front of someone or when someone is in your way)
Pa<u>sen</u>sya na.	*Sorry.*
Ikumusta mo na lang ako kay John.	*Say hello to John for me.*
Pagaling ka.	*Get well soon.*
<u>Ka</u>ya mo 'yan!	*You can do it!*

Polite expressions

When talking to older people, superiors, adult strangers or adult customers, **po'/ho'** (p. 369) is added and **kayo** (p. 54) is used instead of **ikaw/ka**. Examples:

Kumusta?	Kumusta *po'*?
Mabuti naman. *Ikaw*, kumusta?	Mabuti naman *po'*. *Kayo po'*, kumusta?
Magandang umaga.	Magandang umaga *po'*.

Other useful sentences

Anong ibig mong sabihin?	*What do you mean?*
Ano sa tingin mo?	*What do you think?*
Ano sa Tagalog ang "tree"?	*How do you say "tree" in Tagalog?*
Anong ibig sabihin ng "salumpuwit"?	*What does "salumpuwit" mean?*
Pwedeng pakibagalan?	*(Can you speak) more slowly please?*
Hindi' ko maintindihan.	*I don't understand.*
Hindi' ko maalala.	*I can't remember.*
Hindi' ko alam.	*I don't know.*

Opening particles

a

oh, ah

A: **Ka<u>ni</u>nong cell phone 'yan?**	A: *Whose cell phone is that?*
B: ***A*, sa a<u>sa</u>wa ko 'to.**	B: *Oh, this is my wife's.*
A: ***A*, ok.**	A: *Ah, I see.*

ano

so, well (used to introduce a question or a request)

Ano, **<u>si</u>nong na<u>na</u>lo?**	*So, who won?*
Ano, **hindi' ka pa ba tapos?**	*Well, aren't you done yet?*

<u>ba</u>le

so

<u>Ba</u>le, **nandon si Mary....**	*So, Mary was there....*
<u>Ba</u>le **<u>ta</u>tawag ka <u>bu</u>kas?**	*So you'll call tomorrow?*

<u>bwe</u>no

all right (then), very well

<u>Bwe</u>no, **<u>ta</u>tawag ako sa 'yo <u>bu</u>kas.**	*All right, I'll call you tomorrow.*

bweno, bweno
well, well

<u>Bwe</u>no, <u>bwe</u>no, nan<u>di</u>to ka pala.	*Well, well, so you're here.*

e [1]
how about (used to ask about another person or thing, or about another aspect of the situation being discussed)

A: **Ku<u>ma</u>in ka na?**	A: *Have you eaten?*
B: **<u>O</u>o.**	B: *Yes.*
A: *E* **si John?**	A: *How about John?*

e [2]
then

A: <u>Sa</u>bi mo wala' kang cell phone.	A: *You said you didn't have a*
B: **Wala' nga'.**	*cell phone.*
A: *E* **ano 'yan?**	B: *No, I don't, that's right.*
B: **A... sa a<u>sa</u>wa ko 'to.**	A: *Then what's that?*
	B: *Oh... this is my wife's.*

e [3]
but

E <u>ba</u>kit hindi' mo narinig ang alarm?	*But why didn't you hear the alarm?*

e di [1]

so (used to introduce what happened next)

E *di* nandon si Mary... <u>Ta</u>pos lumabas siya... *e di* <u>na</u>sa labas na siya....	*So, Mary was there... and then she went out... so now she's outside....*

e di [2]

then, well then

<u>Sa</u>bi mo gutom ka. *E di* ku<u>ma</u>in ka.	*You said you were hungry. Well then, eat.*
Kung <u>a</u>yaw mo, *e di* huwag!	*If you don't like/want it, fine! If you don't like/want it, then don't do/eat/etc. it!*

ha?

huh? (used to ask someone to repeat or explain what he or she just said)

A: <u>A</u>alis na siya. B: *Ha?* <u>Ba</u>kit?	A: *He/she's leaving.* B: *Huh? But why?*
A: Maganda ba? B: *Ha?* A: Maganda ba? 'Yung T-shirt?	A: *Is it nice?* B: *Huh?* A: *Is it nice? The T-shirt?*

o [1]

so, well

O, anong <u>sa</u>bi niya?	*Well, what did he/she say?*

o [2]

may be used as a non-polite response when someone calls you
(The polite alternatives to **o** are **po'** and **ho'**.)

A: **Marie!**	A: *Marie!*
B: *O?*	B: *Yes? / What?*

See also: **Po'/Ho'** [2] (p. 369)

<u>ta</u>pos

and, and then

Tapos ku<u>ma</u>in sila, *tapos* lumabas sila....	*And they ate, and then they went out....*

Closing particles

a [1]

wow (used to express that you are surprised or impressed by something)

<u>A</u>yos pala 'to *a*.	*Wow, this is cool.*

a [2]

often in combination with **naman**

actually, after all (used to show contrast with what someone said, for instance, when expressing an opposing opinion or correcting someone)

Hindi' *naman* **siya buntis** *a*.	*Actually, she's not pregnant.*

e [1]

you see (used when explaining something or when you hope someone will understand what you're saying)

A: **Ayoko pang kumain. Busog pa 'ko** *e*. B: **A, ok. Akala' ko gutom ka na** *e*.	A: *I don't wanna eat yet. I'm still full, you see.* B: *Oh, ok. You see, I thought you were hungry.*

e [2]

sadly, unfortunately, I'm afraid

Tapos na *e*.	*I'm afraid it's over.*

e [3]

in combination with **nga'**

in fact... even

Marunong na *nga'* **siyang mag-Tagalog** *e*.	*In fact, he/she can even speak Tagalog now.*

ha [1]

used to express friendliness or affection, somewhat like *honey, dear, mate, bro* etc.

Salamat *ha*.	*Thanks, honey/mate/etc.*

ha? [2]

OK?, all right? (used to ask if someone agrees with or understands something)

Mag-ingat ka *ha*?	*Take care, all right?*

ha? [3]

huh? (used to express irritation or impatience)

Anong problema mo, *ha*?	*What's your problem, huh?*
Hindi' ka pa ba tapos, *ha*?	*Aren't you done yet, huh?*

no [1]

you know (used for emphasis or to correct someone)

Pumasa ako *no*!	*I passed, you know!*
Matagal na siyang umalis *no*.	*It's been a while since he/she left, you know.*

no? [2]

huh?, isn't it? etc. (used to ask for agreement or confirmation)

Ang ganda *no?*	*It's so pretty,* **huh?** *It's so pretty,* **isn't it?**

See also: Confirmation questions (p. 389)

o [1]

look! (used when pointing at someone or something)

Ayun *o!*	*There it is!* **Look!**

o [2]

in combination with **naman** or **nga'**
used when asking a favor

Pakitanggal *naman* **nito** *o.*	*Could you remove this,* **please.**

Interjections

Sige. **O sige.**	*OK. / All right.*
Tama'.	*I agree. / Correct.*
Tumpak! **Sinabi mo!**	*Exactly!*
Syempre.	*Of course.*

Grabe!	*Wow! / Oh, my!*
Ano ba 'yan!	*What the heck (is that)! / My goodness! / For goodness' sake! / For crying out loud!* (expresses surprise, confusion or irritation)
Sayang.	*Too bad. / What a pity. / What a waste.*
Bad trip.	*Bummer.*
Aray!	*Ouch!*
Kadiri'!	*Yuck! / Ew!*
Saklolo! **Tulong!**	*Help!*
Dali'!	*Hurry up!*
Yehey!	*Yay! / Yippee!*
Haching!	*Achoo!* (sneeze)
Talaga?	*Really?*
A ganon? **Ganon ba?**	*Is that so?*
Sigurado ka?	*Are you sure?*
Nye!	Used when something turns out to be not as exciting or extraordinary as expected.
Pwera biro'.	*No kidding.*
Pake ko?	*What do I care?*
Wala' akong pake.	*I don't care.*
Malay mo.	*You never know.*

Ay! **Aba!**	*Oh!*
Naku! **Naku po'!** **Naku pu'!**	*Oh! / Oh no! / Yikes!*
Hay naku. **Hay nako.**	*Sigh. / Oh well. / My goodness… / For goodness' sake… / For crying out loud…* (expresses resignation or irritation, depending on the intonation)
Hoy! **Oy!**	*Hey!*
Uy.	*Psst.*
He!	*Shut up!*
este… **a…** **am…**	*um… / er…*

Appendix A:
Spelling system using diacritical marks

An official spelling system that uses diacritical marks for indicating long vowels and final glottal stops was introduced in 1939. Although it is used in some dictionaries and Tagalog learning materials, it has not been generally adopted by native speakers.

The system divides words into four types based on stress and the presence or absence of a final glottal stop.

word type	characteristics	system using diacritical marks	system used in this book
malumay	• stress on penultimate syllable	dalaga sarili matahimik	dalaga sarili matahimik
malumi' (`)	• stress on penultimate syllable • glottal stop at end of word	batà talumpatì dambuhalà	bata' talumpati' dambuhala'

mabilis (ˊ)	• stress on final syllable	isá malakí bulaklák	isa malaki bulaklak
maragsa' (ˆ)	• stress on final syllable • glottal stop at end of word	sampû butikî salitâ	sampu' butiki' salita'

In addition to the above:

Any stressed syllables other than the penultimate and final syllables are indicated by an acute accent (ˊ).

system using diacritical marks	system used in this book
sásama páaralán nagsásalitâ	sasama paaralan nagsasalita'

This book does not use the spelling system using diacritical marks as the system is quite confusing.

Note:

1. The final glottal stop of *malumi* and *maragsa* words only occurs before a pause, such as at the end of a sentence. When not followed by a pause, the final glottal stop is replaced by vowel elongation.

2. The stress on, or vowel elongation in, the final syllable of *mabilis* and *maragsa* words is optional when followed by a pause. When not followed by a pause, there is no vowel elongation in the final syllable of *mabilis* words. In the case of *maragsa* words, there is final vowel elongation, since it replaces the final glottal stop.

See also: Long vowels (stress) and glottal stops (p. 21).

Appendix B: Terminology

term used in this book	other name(s)
Point of Departure (POD)	subject, topic, trigger, focus, theme
News	predicate, comment, focus, rheme
doer	actor, agent, performer
completed	perfective
uncompleted	imperfective
unstarted	contemplated
recently completed	recent perfective

Bibliography

English, Leo James. (1977) English-Tagalog Dictionary. Manila: National Book Store.

---. (1986) Tagalog-English Dictionary. Manila: National Book Store.

Santiago, Alfonso O. and Tiangco, Norma G. (1991) Makabagong Balarilang Filipino. Manila: Rex Book Store.

Schachter, Paul and Otanes, Fe T. (1972) Tagalog Reference Grammar. Berkeley, Los Angeles and London: University of California Press.

Index

449

CPSIA information can be obtained
at www.ICGtesting.com
Printed in the USA
BVHW07s2343250618
519785BV00008B/68/P